Sports Betting to Win

The 10 keys to disciplined and profitable betting

by Steve Ward

HARRIMAN HOUSE LTD

3A Penns Road
Petersfield
Hampshire
GU32 2EW
GREAT BRITAIN

Tel: +44 (0)1730 233870
Fax: +44 (0)1730 233880
Email: enquiries@harriman-house.com
Website: www.harriman-house.com

First edition published in Great Britain in 2011 by Harriman House.

Copyright © Harriman House Ltd

The right of Steve Ward to be identified as the author has been asserted in accordance with the Copyright,
Design and Patents Act 1988.

978-0-857190-39-0

British Library Cataloguing in Publication Data
A CIP catalogue record for this book can be obtained from the British Library.

Printed in the UK by CPI, Antony Rowe

Risk Warning

Gambling is addictive and can lead to serious losses. Please remember that this book cannot and does not
guarantee success – and that no one can. Always gamble responsibly:

- only gamble with money set aside for the purpose, and which you can afford to lose
- do it just for fun or for the challenge, rather than to gain money that you need
- know that you are often very unlikely to win in the long term
- do not chase after losses
- *never* borrow money to gamble.

If you recognise or fear that you or anyone else may have a problem with gambling, please check out the guidance
at **www.gambleaware.co.uk**.

To Sabine, Ollie and Casper

Contents

About the Author

Steve Ward specialises in performance coaching and training, developing people and teams in risk-taking, high-pressure and results-driven environments, helping them to achieve and sustain high performance and to maximise their potential.

He has over 15 years of teaching, training and coaching experience and has worked with elite athletes and teams in over 30 sports, financial traders and institutions across the globe, sports traders, poker players, business leaders and managers and sales teams. Steve co-managed a large team of over 40 professional traders in London, was a consultant to the BBC TV programme *Million Dollar Traders* and is a regular trainer at the London Stock Exchange. He is also the author of *High Performance Trading – 35 Practical Strategies and Techniques to Enhance Your Trading Psychology and Performance*, published by Harriman House in 2009.

Steve has a special interest in the demands of performing in conditions of financial risk and uncertainty and has extensive knowledge and experience of helping people in the financial and sports markets to develop the skills, attitudes and behaviours required to perform with discipline and to maximise their profitability. Utilising techniques and strategies from sports and performance psychology, behavioural finance, stress management, and cognitive, behavioural and solution-focused coaching, Steve provides practical, powerful, easy-to-learn and easy-to-use methods for improving performance.

High Performance Global Ltd

High Performance Global are leading providers of performance coaching and training, working with people and teams in risk-taking, high-pressure and results-driven environments, helping clients to achieve and sustain high performance.

To find out more, visit their website at **www.highperformanceglobal.com** or email **info@highperformanceglobal.com**.

Acknowledgements

There have been many people who have been instrumental in helping me to write this book and I would like to take this opportunity to thank them for their support.

The following people have made key contributions and without them the book would have been far lesser in richness and in value: Bill Esdaile, Matt Finnigan, Peter Webb, Tony Hargraves, Pete Nordsted Compton Hellyer, Keith Sobey, Ian Massie, Wally Pyrah and Steve Taylor. (Further details of all of the above may be found in the core contributor profiles in the Introduction.)

Thank you also to all of you who took the time to complete the *Sports Betting to Win* survey. This provided many insights and ideas for structuring the book to meet the needs of potential readers.

The people at Harriman House have made the writing and publishing of this book as simple and as stress-free as it could have possibly been, and have demonstrated great support and professionalism along the way.

An important thank you goes to the three people who have significantly helped with their emotional support throughout the writing process – my family:

Sabine, my beautiful wife, for plenty of understanding, encouragement and importantly. . . tea.

Ollie, for keeping me company in the office during the long hours of writing.

Casper, for his unbeatable smiles and laughter, the best tonic at the end of a session at the laptop.

Finally, thanks to all the others who have contributed either personally or through the writing of previous books or articles on sports betting, from which I have been able to capture gems of wisdom to pass on in this text.

Preface – Bring Discipline and Professionalism to Your Betting

Sports betting is a huge growth area: the number of opportunities for betting both live and online, the number of sports and the number of markets available, have all increased significantly in recent times, especially since the advent of the betting exchanges. Meanwhile more and more people have moved beyond having 'a light flutter', or betting as entertainment; they now look to trade these markets with the intention of making serious money. And some have managed to create new careers for themselves as part-time and full-time professional sports traders.

This is not a book about sports-betting strategy. It is a book about sports-betting discipline – what it is and how to get it. Discipline is key to long-term sports-betting success. There are plenty of books on betting strategy but little has been written on the area of sports-betting psychology and discipline. Nevertheless, it is the area of betting which causes most people the biggest challenges. Perhaps in the majority of cases of failed bettors, a problem here is what has prevented them from being successful.

> This book does not present winning sports-betting strategies. It presupposes that you have, and know how to devise, such strategies. Instead, and more uniquely, it teaches you how to execute those winning strategies with discipline and professionalism, and helps you to establish a firm psychological foundation for long-term betting success.

This book has been written based on my own experience and expertise as a performance and psychology consultant, coach and trainer in the financial and sports markets. It is also built on the experience and expertise of leading people from within the world of sports betting and from the ideas and thoughts of people actively sports betting across the UK, who assisted in the research I conducted in the *Sports Betting to Win* survey. It was my intention to write something that is both interesting and useful, an easy but engaging read, that provides insights into how to become more disciplined in your betting. Most importantly, I have tried to write something that provides practical steps for you to implement within your own betting.

Whether you bet at the bookies, online, via the betting exchanges, on the spread markets, pre-match or in-running, this book can help you to develop the mindset and the behaviours required to be truly disciplined and to maximise your profits.

Steve Ward

2010

Introduction – Why Do People Lose at Betting, and What Can Be Done About it?

A growing number of people bet on sport each year. Some are casual punters, others more dedicated, whilst an ever-increasing number of people are attempting to join the new breed of professional betting-exchange traders.

The fact is, though, that the majority of people who bet on sport lose money over time; only a very small percentage make profits in the long run.

It used to be worse. The introduction and rise of the betting exchanges has had a positive impact not just on the number of people who are betting on sport, but also on the percentage who are winning. This is down to the more favourable odds they tend to offer – by eliminating the middle man they provide a fairer market (no more 'over round', the bookies' advantage in their calculated odds) – as well as the ability they provide to not just back but also lay, or oppose, selections.

Wally Pyrah of the *Racing Post* has extensive knowledge and vast experience of the betting world. He feels that "the punters have never had it so good. The opportunities for betting, the markets they can bet on, the ability to bet online, access to information, software, availability of statistics and the ability to lay – all give a far greater advantage to punters than they have ever had."

However, despite all of these advantages, the percentage of long-term winners in the sports markets remains very low indeed. Figures of around 10% are commonly offered.

The low success rate in sports betting is interesting and gives rise to three key questions:

1. Why is it that so few people are able to win at sports betting over time?

2. Are there any commonalities in the 10% that do win?

3. Can someone improve their betting performance to become a long-term winner?

Why is it that so few people are able to win at sports betting over time?

"The main challenge to being successful at sports betting is discipline."

– Steve Taylor

Many people who bet are unable to generate a desirable (profitable) return on a consistent basis. In some cases this is in spite of considerable in-depth knowledge and skills. Regardless of how sound their strategies appear (and might actually be), they seem to fall short of their goals when betting.

Why is this?

There are two keys to successful sports betting.

1. Having a betting strategy with an edge, a positive expectancy – one that makes profits when executed consistently over time.

2. The ability to be able to consistently execute the strategy – to be disciplined.

Once you have the first, it is your ability to be able to consistently execute the strategy, to be able to stick to your rules and to stay disciplined regardless of your situation or circumstance, that will ultimately determine whether you are successful or not. Having both a strategy with an edge and the discipline to execute it would put you into quadrant 1 in the diagram below.

Sports betting success quadrants

	Disciplined	Not disciplined
Strategy with an edge	1	2
No strategy/edge	3	4

Where would you place yourself?

For people in quadrant 2, developing discipline is the real key for becoming profitable. For people in quadrants 3 and 4, the challenge is more on developing a strategy that has an edge – and then developing the discipline to go with it.

Why is discipline so difficult?

Betting places you into an arena of risk, uncertainty and financial decision-making. The combination of these three factors presents a great challenge for the human mind and one which I would argue our biological and psychological conditioning is unfortunately not well suited to. To think and behave in a disciplined way means that we must often go against our natural human instincts – and that is simply not easy. To be successful at sports betting, it's my view that you need to think differently: you need to train your betting brain.

If you are to be successful at sports betting, you need to be prepared and able to cope with the range of temptations and pressures that overcome the vast majority of the people who enter the sports markets. Betting presents you with opportunities to make, or

❝ To be successful at sports betting, it's my view that you need to think differently: you need to train your betting brain. ❞

lose, large sums of money in short periods of time. Discipline helps you to make money, keep what you have made and not lose too much when you do lose.

Typical mistakes made by people who lose at sports betting include:

- betting for excitement and fun and not to make profits
- continuing to bet to recover losses
- overconfidence and betting too big
- over betting – betting too frequently
- rationalising bad decisions
- seeking hot tips
- poor understanding of probabilities
- short-term review of results
- betting in states of anger, frustration, greed or fear
- betting when insufficient preparation and research has been done
- being under-capitalised to achieve the returns they want/expect
- not keeping written records of their bets.

Inside view

"I have seen at first hand just how many people lose and how they lose, the mistakes they make – doubling stakes when they have lost, and all the rest of it."

– Ian Massie

Sports Betting to Win research

Here are some responses to the question 'What do you think makes profitable sports betting difficult?' from the *Sports Betting to Win* survey conducted in 2010.

"Maintaining discipline and detachment. Being able to equally accept swings of fortune (either way)."

"Discipline, not getting greedy and keeping your head cool."

"Patience. Falling into the trap of gambling. Researching events."

"Discipline to keep bets at the set size of bank."

"Staying calm when bets go against you."

"Not doing too many bets."

"Getting used to thinking about how to minimise loss as opposed to 'how much will I win?'"

"Discipline. Strict guidelines. Do not gamble. Be patient."

"Being selective in my betting."

There are many factors that affect our betting discipline and decision-making, that can cause us to deviate away from the choices and actions that we know (particularly in hindsight) we 'should' be doing.

Throughout this book you will learn how your natural instincts drive you to behave in ways that are not conducive to profitable betting. And you will learn how you can develop a winning betting brain, and the discipline required to achieve success.

Are there any commonalities in the 10% that do win?

Successful full- and part-time bettors – whilst of course they differ between each other on what they bet on, and how they do it – do share some important characteristics, notably the ability to take losses. They are rigorous in following betting plans, and execute stringent staking and risk-management rules. They have confidence, as well as a readiness, to admit error and take responsibility for it. Taking a long-term view of betting, they try to maximise overall gains rather than focus on short-term victories. They trade for profits and not for the excitement.

Perhaps most of all, the approach that these profitable people take is a *professional* one. This is a key difference from the casual, haphazard and unstructured approach taken by the majority of people in the sports betting world. A key function of this book is to share with you the major disciplines that make up such an approach.

You won't find the answer to successful sports betting on eBay

"Despite those wonder systems you see littered all over the net, and in places like ClickBank and eBay, promising you the earth and delivering nothing, the secret to successful sports betting is research, patience, discipline and confidence."

– Matt Finnigan

Can someone improve their betting performance to become a long-term winner?

Probably the most important part of becoming successful and profitable at sports betting is learning to become disciplined. With discipline you are more effective and consistent at making good betting decisions; without it, the best betting decisions in the world are only one step away from failure. One moment of indecision, or wishful thinking, can negate even the most perfected strategy; and one moment of stubbornness or pride can mutate even the most harmless of losses into a betting-account car crash.

I use the phrase '*learning* to become disciplined' because many of the solutions to the challenges that betting presents can be learned. Sometimes, too, it can be as simple as committing to the key professional betting disciplines, such as preparation and record keeping.

❝ Many of the solutions to the challenges that betting presents can be learned. ❞

However, the process of developing – and, more importantly, ingraining – new behaviours does take time, and it does take effort, so your levels of motivation will be a determining factor in how far you progress. The most successful people in sports betting did not get there by accident.

> *"You do not wander around and then suddenly find yourself at the top of Mount Everest."*
>
> – Unknown

Becoming more successful and profitable

This book has been written to help you to become more disciplined in your betting, to learn the thinking and behavioural patterns that you need to adopt to enhance your performance and as a result to maximise your profitability.

The focus is on developing your ability to make more effective decisions, to stay disciplined and to learn to execute your betting strategy as flawlessly as possible.

If you have the motivation to work on your betting, to put in the effort and hours required, the willingness to learn and to make changes to the way you currently think and behave, then you have the opportunity to become disciplined and profitable. Even taking a few small steps, making some subtle changes to what you currently do, or don't do, will have an impact over time.

I would strongly encourage you to complete the activities throughout the book, especially to take time at the end of each section to make a few notes, ask how it applies to you, and to consider how you will take action. Engaging in the process like this significantly increases your chances of improving your performance as well as enhancing the value and enjoyment you will get from the book.

Core contributors to this book

In writing this book a number of highly successful sports bettors were key contributors, as were several industry experts. Willing sharers of their thoughts, experiences, advice and importantly time, I am very grateful to each of them for their input and wisdom and for allowing me to share it with you, the reader.

Bill Esdaile

Bill Esdaile has worked in the betting and gaming sector as a sports trader and journalist for over 15 years. He has worked for both the *Sporting Life* and *Racing Post* and spent just under ten years at Sporting Index, world leaders in sports spread betting. He left Sporting in 2006 to set up squareintheair.com, his own marketing and PR agency, which specialises in the betting and gaming sector. He edits the betting section of London freesheet *City AM* and contributes to many other leading publications.

www.squareintheair.com

Matt Finnigan

Matt has been a professional sports trader since 2002 and trades football, cricket and tennis on the betting exchanges. Since 2007 he has run a niche but dynamic trading community called 'The X-Club' where members share ideas and thoughts on the 30 trading strategies he devised for the club trading manual *The X-Trader's Guide*.

The concept behind the X-Club is a simple: To develop the individual trader whilst building a successful trading community. Since its inception, Matt has mentored six traders to full-time status.

You can find more about the trading club and other trading products and services that Matt offers by visiting his website at **www.proxtrading.com**.

In 2010 Matt co-wrote two football betting books, the first being *The Essential World Cup Betting Guide 2010* and the second being *The Premier Football Betting Handbook 2010/11*. The book is supported by a website where a full betting analysis is provided on all 380 Premier League matches, with a unique rating system. Check out **www.premier-betting.com**.

Blog: **www.mattfinnigan.com**

Twitter: **www.twitter.com/mattfinnigan**

Facebook: **www.facebook.com/proxtrading**

Email: **matt@proxtrading.com**

Tony Hargraves

Tony started trading in 2004 after a friend requested he find a way to back all events in a match and win regardless of the result, which led to his discovery of Betfair.

Tony lived in Australia until 2008, when he moved with his wife and two daughters to Scotland to be able to trade live sports without having to phone Betfair (internet betting and in-play trading were still illegal in Australia at the time of writing).

Tony became a full-time trader in early 2008 and got heavily involved in the UK trading community, making many friends and great contacts in the trading business, delivering training courses, producing training videos, developing the Racingtraders software and writing. Since 2010 Tony has headed up the Centaur Sports Trading Academy, designing and delivering a range of courses both live and online for people of all abilities, and producing the *Daily Trader*, a trading information sheet.

Tony's main trading focus is on pre-race trading on the UK horse markets, international cricket and football.

info@centauracademy.com

www.centauracademy.com

Compton Hellyer

Compton Hellyer read Business Studies at Trinity College, Dublin, where he developed a keen interest in both golf and racing. His first job was working for a merchant bank in the City in 1969, which he left to go stockbroking. In 1974 he set up his own company to give advice on the financial and commodity markets and ten years later he formed an association with Intercommodities, now GNI. In 1992 Compton founded Sporting Index, which became the world leader in sports spread betting. Sporting Index was sold to the private equity group Duke Street Capital in 2003.

Compton is now chairman of half a dozen small private companies, mostly with some involvement in sport. He is also a member of the Jockey Club and a non-executive director at Epsom Racecourse. Compton managed the Docklands Express syndicate and currently is involved in two horses with Emma Lavelle.

Ian Massie

Ian Massie graduated from the University of Edinburgh with a first-class degree in Chinese before joining Spreadex in 2008. He is now a senior sports trader with the company, compiling odds on sports as diverse as tennis, Formula 1 and American Football. He is also a successful personal gambler, with proven success over the years in both spread and fixed-odds betting. He can be contacted at **ian.massie@spreadex.com**.

Spreadex is the only firm to offer sports spread betting, sports fixed odds betting and financial spread betting from the convenience of one account. Find out more at **www.spreadex.com**.

Peter Nordsted

Pete Nordsted recently finished 25 years of service as an administrator in the Royal Air Force to become a full-time sports trader after studying the Betfair markets in depth for a number of years.

He is the author of *Mastering Betfair* and co-author of the *Premier Betting Handbook* (**www.premier-betting.com**).

As well as being a full-time sports trader he is also the co-director of Sporting Markets Ltd (**www.sporting-markets.com**) and produces the 'Trade on Sports' newsletter, a publication that devises and tests low-risk strategies to be traded on the Betfair markets.

He is the advisor for Trade on Football (**www.tradeonfootball.com**), where he advises customers where to place their money on in-play football markets.

Wally Pyrah

Wally has been involved in the gambling industry for over 35 years. He started his working life with a 21-year stint at Coral Bookmakers, where he became their first in-house sports odds compiler and later their PR director and spokesperson. This was followed by 14 years as the PR and communications director at Sporting Index. Wally was later headhunted by the *Racing Post* to increase the profile of the UK's only racing/sports betting daily newspaper by becoming their spokesperson, and he now appears regularly on TV stations around the world such as Sky News, Sky Sports News, BBC, Channel 4, CNN, CNBC, Bloomberg and Al Jazeera. Regular radio coverage includes Radio 5 Live, Talksport, and Radio 2.

www.racingpost.com

Keith Sobey

Keith Sobey started life as a senior manager for the Audit Commission and as a deputy director of finance for a local authority, before leaving to pursue his passion for horse racing. Since 2000 Keith has been the managing director of the Centaur Group of companies. Centaur has operated highly successful sports investment funds since 2000 and in 2009 opened a new office in the City of London to offer both short and full-time courses in sports trading and gambling. Keith also heads up the successful Centaur bloodstock operation, with over £1 million in prize money accrued and 12 category 1 and 2 greyhound wins.

info@centaurinvestments.com

www.centaurinvestments.com

Steve Taylor

Steve has been involved within the bookmaking/sports betting industry for 30 years both on and off course. He left school and went to work for Ladbrokes, where he received an excellent grounding and he has always remained involved with the bookmaking industry, even including working part-time as a consultant for Independent Bookmakers (both off course and on the greyhound and horse racing tracks).

In 2002 Steve joined Centaur as an analyst and trader. He has been responsible for the client fund trading for the last eight years. He is currently the head trader and broker, a post which involves monitoring and trading on the betting exchanges and liaising on a daily basis with both on and off course bookmakers to trade clients' funds.

Steve is also one of Centaur Academy's training team and *Daily Trader* analysts.

info@centauracademy.com

www.centauracademy.com

Peter Webb

From an early age Peter developed an innate interest in numbers and risk. This was kick started by the simple task of filling out his father's football pools coupon. From his formative work analysing football matches, Peter progressed to financial markets where he furthered his knowledge of pricing and working in risk markets.

In June 2000 Peter had the foresight to become one of Betfair's very first customers and through his pioneering work has gone on to be one of the longest serving and most successful users of betting exchanges ever.

Peter's early participation and innovative thinking resulted in the birth of Bet Angel. This cutting-edge software has completely redefined the capabilities and performance of a whole generation of market participants. It introduced completely new concepts and strategies which opened up possibilities never witnessed before in sports markets; a process that continues to this day.

Peter continues to contribute significantly to his field of expertise and is widely recognised as a leading expert and key participant in his chosen field. He regularly writes for a number of high profile publications as well as appearing in the media. His methodologies draw seminar audiences from around the world and attract invitations to a wide range of industry events and panels.

www.betangel.com

blog.betangel.com

1 Think Differently

"Most people in sports betting are looking at things in the wrong way"

– Peter Webb

In this chapter:

- Thinking differently
- Mindset – the foundation of success
- Key components of the winning mindset
- Training your brain, changing your mind

Thinking differently

"If you are to be successful you need to be prepared to cope with the range of temptations and pressures which overcome most of the people who enter the sports markets."

– Keith Sobey

With a standard-issue human brain – the one that most of us have – achieving success in sports betting is going to be challenging. The human brain has developed around the primary function of survival, and not on making money betting on sports. Most of the behaviours required to make money by sports betting therefore require you to go against your instinctive human urges. To be successful at sports betting you will probably need to think differently, to adopt new beliefs and specific ways of thinking and often to be counter-intuitive.

"To be successful at sports betting you will probably need to think differently."

> ## Interesting
>
> **"We have to change the way that we do things. Not just on the pitch but off it as well. We have to learn to think differently about every aspect of what we do."**
>
> – Clive Woodward, *Winning!*
>
> **Thinking differently is a common trait amongst the most successful people in any field and was a key part of England's 2003 Rugby World Cup success.**

Mindset – the foundation of success

Your mindset is simply a way of thinking that determines your behaviour, your outlook and your mental attitude. For any given set of betting events – wins, losses, setbacks, mistakes – the differentiating factor in how different people respond to them and accordingly the results that they get will be in their mindsets. Your mindset is the middleman between the events that happen to you and your reactions to those events: it is the processor that determines how what goes in comes out. And it can help you to be successful in your sports betting or it can be the barrier to your success.

Our mindset is the 'middle man' that determines how we react to an event

Developing a mindset that supports winning sports betting is ultimately the key to achieving and sustaining consistent profits. Every behaviour, thought, action and feeling comes from within, so although the development of knowledge and skills is essential, equally important in parallel is this development of a winning mindset. It is the foundation which all of your betting behaviours are built upon.

Mindset is the foundation of your betting performance and results

Key components of the winning betting mindset

Here are some fundamental aspects of a winning betting mindset.

1. Take personal responsibility for your betting performance and results

Think back to a time when you had a losing bet or had a bad betting day. Who or what was the cause of the result you got? The bookie? The exchange? The horse? The team? The computer you were using? The room you were in? The weather? Your pet?

One of the most important factors in achieving and sustaining success in betting is understanding and accepting that *you* are responsible for your results. The results that you get in your betting are created by you.

It is easy to find some other cause for your poor performance; to create stories that shift the focus away from yourself and onto external factors – to blame and complain – but in doing this you take yourself out of the learning and development loop. By not taking responsibility for your actions, you do not enable yourself to reflect on what you did and what you could do differently next time – you have disempowered yourself and given control of your betting results to external factors.

Put it into practice: How did I create that?

Taking responsibility for your betting results and asking yourself 'How did I create that?' is a powerful way of ensuring that you enter a learning loop that will move your performance and results forward over time. Even success without this feedback is half-wasted.

2. Adopt a mastery approach

A mastery approach is focused on you striving to become the best that you can be through a process of continual learning and development.

The key elements of a mastery approach are:

- always looking for ways to improve – a growth mindset

- focusing on yourself and your own betting performance and not on others

- embracing mistakes as a part of the learning process

- not liking losses, but learning from them

- not being satisfied with a good result/outcome if your approach was flawed

- accepting 100% responsibility for your outcomes

- focusing on what is controllable.

(Adapted from *The Trading Athlete* by Shane Murphy and Doug Hirschhorn.)

When you adopt a mastery approach, your betting – however it is going – becomes a series of learning opportunities, of chances to improve, to develop new skills, abilities, knowledge and understanding. In this way you are always consolidating your successes and correcting your errors.

Feedback from each bet and each day (winning or losing, good or bad) is seen as being important to development. What some people might perceive as failure, those with a mastery approach see as feedback and an opportunity to learn. You are driven by a desire to improve and become the best bettor you possibly can be; and this intrinsic internal motivation is a key factor in persistence and betting longevity. People with such an approach enjoy their betting and relish the challenges that it presents, and not only because they are likely, over time, to win more dependably than their competitors.

> ### The betting masters embrace mistakes
>
> **"Expect to make mistakes. They are a part of the learning process."**
>
> – Peter Webb

3. Embrace risk

- Do you consider yourself a risk taker?

- Do you accept that a bet has a non-guaranteed probable outcome?

- Do you believe you are taking a risk when you place a bet?

- Have you accepted the possible consequences?

If you are going to embrace risk, then your answers to those questions all need to be a resounding 'YES'. There is a big difference between assuming you are a risk taker because you place bets and fully accepting and embracing the risks that are inherent every single time you have a bet on. Sports betting is a risk-taking activity; calculating and hazarding risks is precisely the means by which you are rewarded. So if you want to be successful, embracing risk is critical. You cannot get good at something if you do not confront with all your energy what it actually is.

Matt Finnigan offers this perspective on risk taking:

> "Most of us are conditioned into thinking that risk is a bad thing – something that should be avoided at all costs. This conditioning does us no favours when trying to be successful in sports betting. It leads us to

seek out situations that offer no risk and to avoid the better opportunities, where the risk is evident but so too are the rewards.

'I must point out that there is no such situation that offers 'no risk', even if you are playing with potential profits.

"As punters we must embrace risk and not be afraid. As participants in the sports markets, we are risk takers. We have to take risks in order to achieve rewards. So we should welcome risk, just as we will welcome the rewards that come with it."

4. Get comfortable with uncertainty

"I laid Roger Federer against Alejandro Falla in a match during Wimbledon 2010 when I had seen him go two sets down. I had read that Federer had never come back from two sets down at Wimbledon. I was more than happy that my money was won and ignored the rest of the match to do other important things. The rest, as they say, is history." *(Federer came back to win the game 5-7 4-6 6-4 7-6 6-0.)*

– Peter Dreyfus, sports trader

Sporting events offer plenty of opportunity for uncertainty and uncertainty is not easy to deal with. Most humans prefer certainty; we fear the unknown. From one perspective, it would be great if in life we knew what was going to happen all the time. Of course, from another it would actually take out some of the challenge, joy and rewards. Many people who bet say that they like the fact that no one day is the same as another, that they would not enjoy being in a job that was predictable each day. In choosing betting for this reason, you also have to accept that what makes betting different every day is the sheer inescapable uncertainty.

"The problem with the future is that it hasn't happened yet."

– Peter Webb

Many people are addressing uncertainty and randomness in their betting by moving towards sports trading approaches via the exchanges – backing and laying, trading in and out, taking profits at pre-chosen prices and not just waiting for the final outcome. This doesn't eliminate uncertainty, though: it simply incorporates it into the very structure of their betting. They, even more than others, need to plan for uncertainty, to look at possible 'what-if scenarios' and to anticipate things going against the run of play.

So preparation is a good discipline to establish, no matter what kind of sports betting you are currently engaged in.

Put it into practice: what are the chances of that?

A key part of dealing with uncertainty is to start to think about events and outcomes in terms of probabilities. Bill Esdaile suggests that few punters really look at events with a mathematical or probabilistic eye and would benefit from simply asking themselves 'what are the chances of that?'

5. Accept the reality that losses are a part of betting

Something that is absolutely key to success in sports betting is accepting the realities of what it is, and what the possible outcomes are of engaging in it. One of those is that you will have losses. Of course you will. You don't want them, and they are definitely bad things, but there is simply no escaping them. They are statistically guaranteed; even the professionals regularly experience them. The key is in how they respond.

Once you have accepted that losses are a part of betting it frees your mind, reduces the tension, and helps to manage your emotions. You cannot be at your best while you are always tense from trying to merely avoid losing. The right attitude is not to simply shrug them off but to evaluate them and learn from them for the future – some losses are just a part of the random outcomes of betting, others are derived through mistakes, lack of knowledge or ill-disciplined behaviours and offer important opportunities for improvement. The best approach is to focus on what needs to be learned from them, rather than the fact that they have happened – and will happen again.

Sometimes the more you try and avoid something the more you are drawn towards it. Have you ever had one of those awkward moments when you have caught the eye of a stranger walking towards you and ended up doing a side-to-side dance with each other?

When Sven-Göran Eriksson took over the England team in 2001 he brought with him sports psychologist Willi Railo. Together the two of them carefully analysed the England side, and observed that they were playing well below their potential because of a fear of failure. A key term coined by Eriksson and Railo that became a philosophy of the side was "Dare to lose to win".

❝ "Dare to lose to win". ❞

In your betting you have to accept that you will lose money sometimes in order to perform to your true potential. It is *managing*, rather than *avoiding*, those losses that is key.

6. Focus on managing risk, not picking winners

"From my time at Sporting Index it became clear that the best sports traders are focused on managing risk first and foremost and not obsessively trying to pick winners. A key question I asked myself in my own betting was 'how can I make my money last longer?'"

– Compton Hellyer

A common error amongst people who are new to sports betting, and one shared by those who are less successful at it, is putting their primary focus on picking winners. The key focus of those who have enjoyed *long-term success* in betting, on the other hand, is on managing their risk and controlling losses.

The lure and attraction of betting to most people is, of course, making money. To achieve this outcome it seems obvious that the key is picking as many winning bets as possible. But this is to mistake wishful thinking for common sense. Naturally, you need an 'edge' – a well researched, plausible strategy or positive expectation behind each bet – but you also need to be aware of your own fallibility and the law of averages. Since you cannot always win, even with the most percipient betting approach, you need to deal with risk and losses with ruthlessness and speed.

By learning to manage risk and control losses as a priority, you create longevity. You also make your betting a continual learning process for yourself. This keeps you in the game and keeps you improving.

"Rule 1": Winning is less important than not losing

"Rule 1 on my courses is that winning is less important than not losing.

"There have been many times when a team I have backed had a clear lead with just minutes to go, have been trading at 1.05 or thereabouts, and have gone on to lose. So I now always hedge my trades, win or lose; and sure, it costs me a few pounds each time I was right with my assessment, but it saves me hundreds of pounds on those times that they go on to lose after being in a seemingly unbeatable position. I had to learn to let go of 'what could have been' and just face what is in front of me and deal with that. I had to get used to winning £30 with no risk of losing as opposed to winning £200 but only if I was right. That took three years to master."

– Tony Hargraves

7. Bet for profits not excitement

"If people want to become successful at sports betting, the first question they must ask themselves is why am I doing this? Is it for fun and entertainment, or is it to make profits? Becoming successful at sports betting is not easy and requires a professional approach. In my experience not many people take this approach and do what is required to be profitable in the long run. I am always surprised by how few 'serious' punters actually know basic information about their betting such as their turnover or win/loss ratio."

– Keith Sobey

Are you betting for excitement and fun or for profits?

This, as Keith has stated, is a fundamental question you must ask yourself. The ways in which you behave and the performance and outcomes of your betting will vary greatly depending on your answer, because your motivations are a driver of your behaviour.

For people who are betting for excitement and fun, their approach will be more casual, with less inclination to prepare or to record and evaluate results, less structure, and with decisions based on creating a buzz rather than a 'profit'.

For people who are betting to make money, betting is a business. A professional approach is adopted as a result of that, and decisions are made to maximise profits and minimise losses – not to meet emotional needs of excitement, socialising or fun.

8. Emphasise process over results

What is more important: having a winning bet or knowing that your betting approach was disciplined and applied correctly?

What is most important: the result or the process?

For the typical punter, it is all about the *result* and the buzz they get from that result when it goes their way. For the professional, the *process* is key – doing the right things at the right time for the right reasons. The 'buzz' comes from the feeling of knowing that they did everything possible to get the best possible result. This is a mastery approach, and, unlike a punter, a professional trader would not feel satisfied with a winning bet if the process that led to it was flawed. I call this approach to performance a focus on 'flawless execution'.

The key is doing the right thing at the right time for the right reasons. Focus on the flawless execution of your betting strategy.

Ultimately, at some level, most people's betting success will be measured by the amount of money they are making or losing. However, it is important, and it is a trait of the best people in sports betting, to be able to separate out making money and betting well.

Is it possible to plan a bet and execute it well – yet lose?

Is it possible to do no planning and have a random long shot punt – and win?

In the short term there can be little direct correlation between the quality of your betting process and strategy and the outcomes that you get. However, in the long term there is a significantly greater chance of success where you apply a disciplined approach to your betting. Many people are unsuccessful at sports betting because they put too much focus on money

> **❝The key is doing the right thing at the right time for the right reasons. Focus on the flawless execution of your betting strategy.❞**

and it takes them away from the strategies, rules and the decisions they know they should be making.

Placing your focus on the process of betting well – the process of success – and trusting in yourself to stick to your process through good times and bad is the desired outcome.

Put it into practice: flawless execution

Make a list of the key actions that contribute to you having the best chance of making a successful bet. Focus on completing these actions every time you bet – make them automatic.

9. Take a long-term view

"Get rich slowly."

– J. D. Roth

If you are looking to make money from sports betting, then you need to play for the long term and accept the short-term risks.

This is quite a challenge; as we have discussed, humans are hard-wired for short-term reward and short-term thinking. Would you rather have £5 today or £6 tomorrow? Most of us would take the £5 today.

Our needs for instant gratification are great and betting allows opportunities for us to meet that need, though not always with the desired outcome. And that *undesired* outcome can easily lead to unplanned, rash, further bets – as indeed can the euphoria of a betting victory. In other words, a short-term view can shortly lead to disaster.

Therefore you have to condition yourself to be able to bet according to your process. Flawless execution, not the old-fashioned 'light flutter', gets to the very heart of successful modern sports betting. You must not be reactive in the light of your recent, short-term, performances, whether down or up. Humans have a tendency to make decisions based on what has just happened to them (called the recency bias), but keeping the long-term view in mind instead is key.

It is also important to understand that in any small sample, and in the short term, 'luck' or randomness may be a significant factor; and that only over time, as a sample size increases, will the true results of your betting strategy become evident, and your skill, knowledge and discipline take precedent.

10. Enjoy small wins

"Some people only ever seem to want to hit the sexy six, and not take the singles."

– Compton Hellyer

When you first start betting, a win, no matter how small, feels great. But after a while you do not seem to get the same sense of satisfaction from those same-sized stakes and wins. You feel the desire to take greater risk and aim for bigger wins. As your wins get bigger and bigger (if you are so lucky), you feel better and better. Each time you win with a bigger amount, you get a release of dopamine, the pleasure chemical, in the brain – and the feeling is very powerful. Smaller, and even equal-sized wins, no longer provide the same 'buzz'.

The same phenomenon is seen, for instance, in bungee jumpers who seek ever-higher and ever-riskier jumps, and by extreme sports athletes who seek to perform bigger tricks, ride bigger waves, BASE jump... each time, greater risk needs to be taken to produce the same old amount of dopamine.

Progression in sports betting is key, and a part of this is taking more risk; however, it is critical to understand how your need for a 'dopamine moment' can cloud your decision making, and how you can become obsessed with only wanting big wins. This is desperately hazardous, and will sooner or later be rewarded with a loss many times more grievous than necessary or inevitable.

Many successful sports bettors achieve their results by having multiple small winners that outweigh their small losers. They are risk managers. They enjoy the process of winning and get their buzz from seeing their bank balance, rather than their risk, grow over time. They are not interested in one-off short-term fixes. In *Enhancing Trader Performance*, Brett Steenbarger strongly urges traders to adopt a methodology that produces smaller winners *and* losers to avoid the 'trauma' that large losses have on us psychologically. He relates the impact of these extreme wins and losses to the trauma of car crashes and other psychologically stressful life events.

If you need excitement, adrenaline and dopamine in your life and want to be successful with your betting then look for other ways to meet that need. In your sports betting, the figure to get thrilled over is your growing profits column over time, rather than the amount that hangs on a particular wager.

11. Adopt a positive attitude to money

Risk and uncertainty are two key psychological challenges for making good decisions. Money is the third one.

Money can have serious emotional and psychological effects on people and the decisions they make. How you think about money can affect how you bet and the outcomes you get. I remember once coaching someone who appeared to be quite a competent trader and was definitely able to make good money, but seemed to keep giving it all back in a cycle of ups and downs and continual frustration. As we worked together over a few weeks it transpired that his general attitude to money was that it was "easy come and easy go". He had quite a carefree attitude to cash – and though he by no means had a carefree attitude to his trading, this attitude was nevertheless crossing over and playing out there for all to see.

Your beliefs about money are important. How you view your betting account, how you feel about the money you are making or losing, and whether you see betting as involving *numbers* or *cash*, will all stem from it. Ideally this should be: professionally unemotional, and cold, hard, real-life cash! Matt Finnigan explains how he overcame his own particular challenge:

> "One of my biggest hurdles in making the transition from knowing how to trade to becoming a successful sports trader was learning how to respect money.

> "The problem that I had with my trading bank was that it wasn't real money to me, just numbers on a screen. And in the early days this led me to make all kinds of rash decisions.

> "I was conditioned to dealing with cash in my hand rather than a balance on a screen; the latter felt unreal. I overcame this by putting some cash in a box (a decent amount) and placing it near where I traded. I then had something tangible to hold every time I got the urge to do something rash with those mere numbers on a screen!

"This certainly helped me become more respectful of my trading bank. Even today I still have some cash in a box nearby, just in case that demon rears its ugly head again. You should also remember that your winnings aren't actually won till you've sent them from your bookmaker's account to your bank account."

12. Believe you can be a winner

This final component of the ideal betting mindset is definitely of the 'last but not least' variety. Whilst it may be number 12 here, it is probably one of the most important factors of all.

1. Do you believe it is possible to win at sports betting?

2. Do you believe that you are able to win at sports betting?

These are two fundamental questions that you must ask yourself.

Many people feel that there is only one winner in betting and that is the bookie. This is a common perception; and amongst those who choose to continue to bet at the bookies without structure or discipline, it is probably true.

However, since the advent of sports spread betting, and the betting exchanges in particular, the betting landscape has changed dramatically. The balance of power has shifted, and with it so have the opportunities for profitability and success. The bookies' key advantages of the over round and being the only ones with the ability to lay have both been removed. In parallel, the internet has also meant that the availability of sports information and data has significantly increased; so getting an edge in your sports betting is that much more possible.

If you want to be a winner you need to change your mind

"The main challenge to being successful in sports betting is modifying your mindset from that of a loser into that of a winner. It's human nature to belong to the crowd and the general perception towards betting is that the only winners are the bookmakers. That's not really a helpful attitude to have if you actually want to beat them at their own game."

– Matt Finnigan

Having interviewed people such as Compton Hellyer, Ian Massie and Wally Pyrah from inside the gambling industry, it is clear that thinking in part like a bookie and not a punter is critical to sports betting success.

Bookies know how punters think and the betting industry encourages and entices the behaviours that will leave most customers parting with their hard-earned cash for no return. Being aware of and avoiding the traps and temptations presented to you – including fun bets and online casinos – and utilising all of the resources you can to give yourself a competitive advantage, must be your goal. This is a key plank in creating the conditions and opportunities for sports betting success.

Success in sports betting is possible, and you may be able to achieve it yourself, but it will take time and effort, it will take a professional approach, it will take discipline.

It will require you to change your mind.

Training your brain, changing your mind

The first step in training your betting brain to become a winning one is to understand what your mindset is right now: how you think, the thoughts you have and the beliefs and perceptions they create – as we looked at in the first part of this chapter.

The second step is to develop an awareness of your mindset from *a betting perspective*. How do your thoughts and beliefs play out in your betting, and how could they, and your betting, be improved?

 Review: how is your current mindset?

Take a moment to reflect on your own betting mindset.

Review your betting performances and results and see if you can identify how your thinking has helped you or worked against you.

Reflect on decisions you have made. What were you thinking that led to that decision?

Where are your mindset strengths?

Where could you become stronger?

Finally, the third step is to take control: to actively create and develop your winning mindset. This requires you firstly to want to change and then to have a process to actively adopt the ways of thinking of a successful and profitable person; noticing your thoughts, to be aware of when your thinking is limiting you, and to change your thoughts to more empowering ones.

Put it into practice: winning mind training programme

Behaviours and ways of thinking are conditioned through what we say, what we do and what we reward.

SAY: Write down a key word or phrase that represents the way of thinking you want to have. Repeat these as often as possible to make them automatic.

- I fully accept that losses are a part of my betting.

- I am a risk taker. I embrace and manage my risk to maximise my profits.

- I am focused on learning to increase my earning.

- I am a winner when I execute my strategy flawlessly.

DO: Focus on actually doing the behaviours that the way of thinking would produce.

REWARD: Reward yourself by feeling good when you have been disciplined and thought like a winner. Attach negative feelings to when your thinking and discipline was that of a loser.

Taking action

Now you have read this section, take time to write a few notes, the key points, then consider how they apply to you in your own sports betting, before finally thinking about how you can take action.

Notes

How does this apply to me?

How can I take action?

2 Bet for Profits, not Excitement

"If you treat betting as a hobby it will remain just that. If you harbour ambition of being a professional you need to be prepared to put the effort in."

– Matt Finnigan

In this chapter:

- What is your motivation for betting on sport?
- What is your betting type?
- Uncovering your core betting motivations
- Creating inner drive for long-term success

What is your motivation for betting on sport?

One of the most important questions you must ask yourself is:

"Why am I sports betting?"

And then consider:

"What do I want from my sports betting?"

▶ Review: betting motivation

List the reasons why you currently bet on sports.

....

....

....

....

.... ✎

What do you want from your betting?

....

....

....

....

.... ✎

Many people bet on sport but their motivations, and as a result their outcomes and profitability, vary. Your motivation is a key driver of your betting behaviour and so understanding why you are betting and the likely consequences of this on your behaviour are key.

Ultimately, and in very simple terms, people are betting for one of two reasons – either for fun and entertainment, or for profits.

Betting for profit – a professional approach

The sports-betting professional is focused solely on making profits. He is not in it for fun, excitement or for adrenaline surges – although he may experience these at times and enjoy them, they are not his primary motivation. He carries out considerable research and operates a proven strategy, with a positive expectancy, in a disciplined manner in order to generate an annual income sufficient to meet his desired outcomes.

This approach to betting is the most successful. However, it requires a strong commitment to developing the skills, knowledge and behaviours required. And discipline is its cornerstone.

Betting for entertainment and fun

Entertainment betting can be hugely enjoyable and can also result in profits. The gambling activities of the vast majority of people who bet on sport fall into this category.

Examples of entertainment betting are:

- going racing socially and having a small bet on each race
- having a bet every Saturday on the horses, football, or other events
- watching a football match or golf tournament on television and betting on the outcome.

There is absolutely no problem *per se* with this entertainment – betting can be an enjoyable hobby when controlled. The danger with this type of betting exists when it takes place without budgetary and emotional control; people's financial stability and personal life can be put at risk. Betting creates powerful emotions within people and these can lead to quite destructive behaviours.

What is your betting type?

It is important to know why you are betting and to understand what the implications of this are. Take a look at the six betting types below (adapted from the 'six types of gambler' devised by Keith Sobey of Centaur).

The six betting types

1. Professional

2. Semi-professional

3. Punter

4. Entertainment

5. Casual

6. Addict

Look at the profiles below and see which best fits you.

1. Professional

Definition

Full-time professional deriving most if not all of their income from betting.

Motivation

To maximise profitability. Importantly they will often have stronger and deeper motivations lying beneath the monetary outcomes e.g. freedom, choice, opportunity.

2. Semi-professional

Definition

Typically someone who is employed full-time and is sports betting as an additional income or is working towards being able to become a full-time professional. They will adopt a systematic approach to betting, which generates (some) profit without involving the same degree of time and research as a full-time professional may put in, typically by specialising on a particular category of sports betting.

Motivation

To maximise profitability and generate a part-time income or develop the ability and opportunity to be able to bet full-time.

This is perhaps the most realistic goal for most people in that betting can become a very enjoyable and financially rewarding part-time pursuit. This can actually be the ideal for most people, as it allows the comfort and security of a day job and the chance to generate an additional income on the side. Full-time professional betting is not for everyone.

3. Punter

Definition

The punter is defined here, and throughout the book, as a betting regular who does not adopt a professional approach in terms of running a trading business, thorough research, record keeping, and continual learning.

Motivation

Excitement and fun come before profits – even though the punter may not admit it. There can also be a social motivation of meeting with like-minded people at the betting shop or on course.

Visit your local betting shop and you will see many people who fit this description; it often involves an inability to leave the shop each day without, at some point, putting their entire funds at risk.

4. Entertainment

Definition

People who bet on sporting events occasionally – and maybe even regularly – but with entertainment as their focus. Typically this includes people who go to the races and have a small bet on each race or people who bet on the football each weekend.

Motivation

Fun, entertainment, social.

5. Casual

Definition

Covers most of the wider population who like to have a bet on the Grand National or on a major sports event such as a World Cup.

Motivation

One-off bit of fun every now and then.

6. Addict

Definition

"Persistent and recurrent maladaptive gambling behaviour that disrupts personal, family, or vocational pursuits..." (*American Psychiatric Association's Diagnostic and Statistical Manual of Mental Disorders*, 4th Edition (APA, 1994).)

Motivation

There can be many underlying causes of addictive gambling, including chasing to recover losses, looking for a rush, an escape from daily life, a preoccupation with gambling and biological biases.

If you feel that sports betting may be an addiction for you then you should seek help. Contact **www.gamcare.org.uk**.

* * *

Knowing which type you fall into is important, particularly when it comes to your motivations and what you want to achieve from your sports betting. If you are betting for fun and excitement and not adopting a professional approach then it is unrealistic to expect consistent and profitable returns over time. Likewise if you are betting to make profits and adopting a professional approach, then you need to let go of any primary need for fun, excitement and adrenaline rushes.

Uncovering your core betting motivations

Below is a great exercise to complete to make you more aware of what your core betting motivations are, to help you to clarify exactly what you want from your betting, and (if appropriate) to motivate you to adopt the particular approaches that will bring success.

 Review: uncovering your core betting motivations

- Why did you start betting on sports? (Or, if not actively betting, why do you want to start betting on sports?)

- What was it about sports betting that particularly attracted you?

- What do you want from your sports betting? What would that give you?

- What do you enjoy about sports betting? What do you not enjoy?

- Why is sports betting important to you?

It is important to understand why you are betting, what your style of betting is, and what the likely financial impact of that is. Your expectations should be in line with your motivations and actions. For some people, sports betting is a hobby which can be quite serious; for others it is a hobby but very casual. For some it is a chance to top up their main income or even a pension, and for others it is their full-time profession. Whatever your motivation, being clear about it and setting your expectations accordingly is very important.

Creating inner drive for long-term success

For those of you who are committed to achieving long-term, consistent profits, your motivation levels are critical. Motivation is the fuel of success – it is what keeps you going. Sports betting has many ups and downs and your motivation will be tested over and over again.

Motivations can be classified as being either intrinsic (internal) or extrinsic (external). Intrinsic motivations are those that come from within and include feelings of success or pride, a desire to achieve a goal. Extrinsic motivations include money, material possession, reward and praise from others.

Take a look at your motivations from the exercise above and classify each of them as being either intrinsic or extrinsic. What is your balance like across the two types?

Research in performance psychology has shown that people with strong intrinsic motivations tend to be more persistent and achieve more than those whose motivations are more extrinsic. It is a useful idea to identify and connect with a strong internal source of motivation – a core driver – one that really has a sense of meaning and purpose to you; and stay focused on this.

Core driver: owning time

"When I made the decision to trade full time, it wasn't about the money but the opportunity of owning time – and that's the biggest commodity of all."

– Matt Finnigan

**Put it into practice:
reinforcing your motivation and commitment**

- Make a list of your core betting motivations – the primary reasons you are betting.

- How will these motivations and your commitment be demonstrated? What action will you take? E.g. always doing preparation before betting, keeping records.

- Read through the list regularly to reinforce your motivation and commitment to achieving success in sports betting.

Taking action

Now you have read this section, take time to write a few notes – recording the key points – then consider how they apply to you in your own sports betting. Finally, think about how you can take action.

Notes
....

How does this apply to me?
....

How can I take action?
....

3 Prepare to Win

"Victorious warriors win first and then go to war, while defeated warriors go to war first and then seek to win."

– Sun Tzu (from *The Art of War*)

In this chapter:

- Know the game
- Betting success factors
- Developing a betting plan
- Creating a betting strategy
- Warming-up – PREParation

Know the game

I remember meeting a person on a betting course I was teaching who told me how he had lost over £5,000 in the first few months of his betting. He said that he then stopped and took some time out to consider things, and his biggest realisation was that he didn't *really* know much about the sports betting markets: how to truly use each aspect of the betting exchange, what each market fully involved, and – most importantly – what the risks were at any one time or bet. He knew just enough to be dangerous – to himself.

I asked him what he did for a living. He replied that he ran a very successful business. I asked him how he had created such success with his business, and he told me about how he had found a potential niche to exploit, performed lots of research, had to undergo some training and further education and then devised his business plan, before seeking funding and support for his venture. I asked him if he felt he had been thorough in his preparation before actually launching his business. Yes, he replied, you have to be – the risk of not being prepared is too great.

I then asked him to reflect on what his approach to his betting had been like in comparison to his approach to his business start-up. Obviously they had been very different.

Many people get sucked into sports betting without having a really good understanding of what they are getting into and what the potential risks and associated costs are. I have, as a result of this, met many people who have lost a lot of money; and in most of those cases, those losses could have been reduced or even avoided.

Betting is too often treated casually, or as a hobby, even by those who are trying to make consistent profits from it. To increase your chances of success, your betting should be treated as a business and then run accordingly.

Running your sports betting like a business

What does this mean? Well in essence there are several key components that need to be in place. Some have been covered in depth already, whilst others are covered later. Boiled down to their essence, they are:

- **Mindset** – you adopt the belief that your sports betting is a business and not a hobby. This is key to enabling you to act appropriately both in the moment and at more strategic times.

- **Business plan** – in essence your betting plan is your business plan. It must be a document that not only outlines how you might make money one day (or by one bet) but what your overall, long-term, daily activity can expect to bring home: what storms it will have to weather, what time frames it will be organised by, what are its (short-, medium-, long-term) targets, its core justifications and when and how you will review it.

- **Balance sheet** – all companies have a balance sheet that shows income and expenditure and either the current profit or loss. For sports betting you will want to look at the income derived from your betting, minus the expenditure of commission paid, the cost of any trading or analysis software you use, information feeds or membership groups you subscribe to, and any training or coaching you have (or have had).

- **Working conditions** – what hours will you work? How much holiday will you take? Are there any particular routines or regular tasks, such as your research and evaluation, that you will commit to doing? These are important questions to ask yourself. It can be all too easy to make your sports betting a very casual affair. And it's just as easy to say that it is a business but *not* act in accordance with that. Getting the balance right between freedom and focus is the key.

- **Development** – how will you grow your business over time? What are your plans for growth and how will you achieve them? What key actions need to be taken? Who do you need to become? What skills or knowledge do you need to develop? How will you get them? How will you increase the success and profitability of the business over time?

Professional sports betting requires a professional businesslike approach

"Before you go into any business you need to go through a detailed planning process. For example, in the retail sector, you would not commence until you had thoroughly researched environmental, demographic and financial considerations."

– Keith Sobey

Know your stuff

If you want to be successful at sports betting you need to understand what you are getting into and you need to prepare yourself accordingly. Going into the sports betting arena with limited knowledge and understanding is a recipe for disaster. Being well informed, planned and prepared will help you to create the opportunity to win in the long run.

There are five key areas which you need to focus your knowledge and understanding on:

1. What it takes to be successful in sports betting – what factors help or limit success?
2. The fundamentals of the betting industry and how bookies, spread companies and betting exchanges operate.
3. The sports and markets that you are going to be trading.
4. Betting strategies, approaches and risk management.
5. Yourself and your betting brain – what you do and why you do it.

No earning without learning

"It is important to know what you are doing and to understand what you are betting on and how those bets are made up."

– Ian Massie

"Learn how the markets work, what they react to and why."

– Tony Hargraves

Many people seem to enter the sports betting world looking for a get-rich-quick solution, only to find that they get a get-poor-quick problem. There seems to be an illusion that sports betting is easy and that anyone can be successful at it.

Get rich slowly

Imagine if you saw these adverts in your local paper. What would your thoughts be?

Would you be rushing to sign up? Would you take them seriously?

I have been very fortunate to speak and work with many successful people in sports betting. The one common factor in all of their cases was that they survived the learning curve and got to the earning curve through sustained focus and effort *over time*. We've touched on what this means in terms of mindset in previous chapters. What does it mean in terms of practical preparation?

❝ They survived the learning curve and got to the earning curve through sustained focus and effort over time. ❞

Important advice for beginners

"Practise at a low level until you are confident in what you are doing. I started off by putting £100 into my Betfair account and traded and practised until I had eventually lost it. It was the best and most important £100 I have ever spent on my betting."

– Steve Taylor

"Study, paper trade, then when you gain experience and confidence go to real money trading."

– Diego Cassanova BTC www.sportsarbitrages.com

For everyone, getting to the stage where you have acquired sufficient experience and gained the required level of competence is a primary goal. How long is this period? How long is a piece of string? It will be different for different people. We are all unique with our own particular set of circumstances.

However, we are talking months and years here, not days. In his book *Outliers*, which examines what it takes to become highly successful, Malcolm Gladwell talks of the "ten thousand hours" that it takes to achieve this. In *The Road to Excellence*, K. Anders Ericsson quotes the "ten years" that acquiring expertise takes. And there is, of course, the old adage that 'it takes ten years to become an overnight success'. Pete Nordsted has observed a common tendency in the typical punter to not put in the sufficient work required, to be lazy, and to instead flit from idea to idea and system to system.

Betting success factors – stacking the odds in your favour

"Create the conditions and opportunity to win."

– Yehuda Shinar, *Think Like a Winner*

There are specific factors that can accelerate and sustain your progress, and increase your chances of success – what we might call *betting success factors*. Building these into your preparation is very important. Most people entering sports betting display behaviours and actions that are completely contrary to this approach. They soon become financial casualties.

Here is a list of some of the key betting success factors, most of which are covered in more detail elsewhere within the book. I've flagged them all at this stage, as it is in *preparation* that you must begin to bear them in mind.

- Motivation – critical to keeping you going and sustaining effort

- Adopting a professional approach based on making profits – you are running a sports-betting business

- Level of knowledge, understanding and skill – betting, the markets, yourself

- A suitable betting strategy with a positive expectancy

- Strong risk management and staking strategies

- Sufficient capital/betting bank

- Resilience – psychological, physical and financial – to get through the tough times

- Regular evaluation and analysis of your betting results

- Training, coaching and mentoring – high quality, organised and structured

- The ability to learn and adapt and to *continually* do so

- Positive beliefs, attitudes and perceptions about yourself, betting, success and money/wealth

- Love of/enthusiasm for betting

- Time/immersion – time to learn, practise and bet

- Support – friends, family, colleagues

- Contacts, network and information sources that can support you and maybe give you some edge.

 Review: betting success factors

Take a look at the list of betting success factors.

Which do you have already in place?

Are there areas where you could develop and enhance your performance?

What do you need to work on and develop next in order to continue developing your betting?

Developing a betting plan

"If you fail to plan, you plan to fail"

– Old saying (uknown)

In order to achieve success in anything you need to have a good plan laid out before you start. Can you imagine starting a new business without a business plan? Planning and preparation underpin your performance. Betting is no different. It is absolutely essential that you develop a plan and a strategy before you start betting.

"Have a plan. Decide on the sport you will bet on; what you will focus on; your staking system; prices and rules; open a separate betting account; write down every bet."

– Compton Hellyer

You need to develop a plan that, amongst other things, considers:

- Why are you betting?

- What sports will you bet on? (And will you only bet on certain markets within those sports?)

- How you will bet on them – what strategies you will use?

- What information and analysis will you use?

- What software and tools will you use to assist you?

- How will you manage your risk – what is your staking plan?

- How will you stay disciplined?

- How will you evaluate your betting results?

- When will you be doing your betting? (Evenings, weekends, etc.)

- What advantages (edge) do you have in the market (knowledge, skills, execution, psychological)?

- What strengths do you have? How will you utilise them?

- What weaknesses do you have? How will you overcome them?

- What contingency plans do you have – for a losing day; a series of losing bets/days?

- How will you manage the mental and emotional aspects of betting?

- What are the costs of betting – fixed and variable?

It is important that this plan is a reflection of you, your betting philosophy, goals and motivations. Bill Esdaile stresses this and the importance of being your own person and developing your own strategy, ignoring tipsters and the magic-system sellers and developing your own skills, abilities, knowledge and most importantly judgement.

Backtesting your strategy

"To be successful you need to backtest a strategy to ensure it is profitable, then make sure you have the necessary funds to carry it through; and then you have to have the discipline to implement your plan without exception."

– Pete Nordsted

Put it into practice: creating your sports-betting plan

Really do take the time to sit down and write out your betting plan. Think of it like writing a business plan that you would have to present to your bank manager or financial backer.

The clearer and more defined your plan is, the more likely you are to be able to consistently follow it and evaluate your progress against it.

Review and update your betting plan as time goes on, and in line with the progress you are making, as well as any changes to your betting approaches that you have made or that have occurred in the sports markets.

Creating your betting strategy

Your betting strategy is the finer detail of how you actually select bets, place them and manage risk/stakes. It defines what sports and markets you will trade and how you will trade them. Developing a strategy with a positive expectancy (i.e. which returns profits over time when consistently executed – see box below for details of how to calculate expectancy) is the first and most fundamental goal in betting – without this you are floating aimlessly in a generally haphazard way and consistency will be hard to come by: except that you may find yourself consistently losing money.

The two keys to successful betting

Calculating expectancy

Expectancy is a measure of the expected return per bet based on the sample size that you use in the data. If the number that comes out is positive then the strategy is said to have a positive expectancy, whilst on the flip side if the number is negative the strategy has a negative expectancy.

```
(Percentage of winners in decimal format x average winning
bet in monetary terms) - (Percentage of losers in decimal
format x average losing bet in monetary terms)
```

E.g. For a person who wins 60% of the time and at an average of £100, and who loses 40% of the time at an average of £50, the expectancy would be:

```
(0.6 x £100) - (0.4 x £50) = £60 - £20 = £40
```

The ability to develop a betting strategy is a skill that takes time to learn. It is common for newer entrants to sports betting to adopt a standardised approach utilising a strategy or style that someone else has taught them, perhaps in a book or on a course. Over time you should be looking to refine and individualise your betting style and the sports and markets you bet on. The process of going from a standardised approach to an individualised one is a part of the pathway to betting success.

When you are developing your strategy you should be always be looking to create (or sustain) an edge, a competitive advantage, that enables you to make money from betting.

If you are currently betting, ask yourself:

What is my edge? What is my competitive advantage?

The sports markets are dynamic and ever changing, so over time you will need to be able to adapt your style and strategy in response to this. Having the ability to develop a strategy is a key factor in creating longevity in your betting career.

> ## Make hay while the sun shines
>
> **"There is a finite time that you have an edge for and it is up to you to exploit it for as long as you can and to try and get as much money as you can."**
>
> – Ian Massie

Peter Webb feels that most people do not think enough about how the markets are changing and developing. Their edge reduces over time, till it eventually disappears or shrinks to uselessness – leaving them with the challenging situation of having to develop a new strategy whilst also trying to sustain performance and profitability from a serious low ebb.

Peter's solution to this problem is to spend one to two hours per day looking at market trends and evaluating data to test future strategies. His approach is very proactive and enables him to transition through changes in market conditions with low stress and sustained profitability.

"In warfare there are no constant conditions. He who can modify his tactics in relation to his opponent will succeed and win."

– Sun-Tzu, *The Art of War*

Specialise to get an edge

Are all people suited to and therefore likely to excel in the same jobs or careers? Are all people suited to and therefore likely to excel in the same sports? Are all people suited to and therefore likely to excel at playing the same instrument? The answer, of course, is no. So are all people suited to and therefore likely to excel in the same style of betting? Of course not.

But it's not just a matter of finding what you're good at. Diversifying is also a means of finding those opportunities that others have overlooked. There are many different sports and markets to trade and many different ways in which to bet on them. Compton Hellyer supports this view from his extensive industry experience.

"Focus," he says, "on mastering one sport and not on trying to bet on everything. Knowledge is an edge. Focusing on minority sports can give you an advantage, as these are sports where the bookmaker will most likely have their junior odds compilers working on them; the pricing will have more discrepancy."

Specialising in specific sports and market areas can have a number of other benefits:

- it can save you time, as you do not have to evaluate all sports/events

- inside knowledge on team selection from sports websites can often put you ahead of the market

- the weaknesses of rival bettors are more easily exploited in under-populated markets.

Getting an edge with a minority sport

"One well-known trader at Sporting Index had a phenomenal record based on trading Rugby League, where his expert knowledge, mathematical thinking and trading ability were too great for the junior odds compilers at the bookies and less-informed and less-disciplined punters on the exchanges."

– Wally Pyrah

Hitting the sweet spot

Punters often seem to be conducting a search for a holy grail that will grant them instant wealth from sports betting. Big profits with little effort is the aim – hence pursuing tipsters, the latest betting system or the promises of some automated program.

The secret is that there is no magic formula to success in sports betting. Well, that's not quite true. There is. But, critically, *the magic is different for everyone.*

There is no magic system, but there is a system, a style and an approach that will work best for you. Finding this is the holy grail. And, of course, the markets are dynamic, so it is unlikely that the grail will remain in your hands forever – it must be repeatedly pursued.

Specialising within a specialism

"The more you specialise in a sport, the better. You can go further, too, and focus on a particular aspect of that sport – for example, in horse racing, flat rather than jumps; and then you may opt to only focus on two-year-old races; and so on."

– Bill Esdaile

The sweet spot

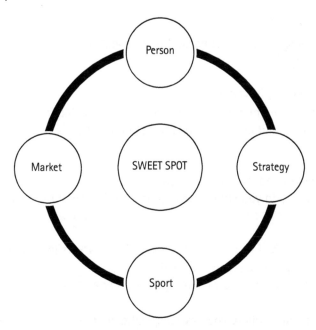

The sweet spot occurs when the blend of the person betting, their strategy and the sport and markets they bet on matches up as perfectly as possible – providing the opportunity for maximum profitability.

A question I am often asked is 'How do I know if I am betting on the best market and style for me?' The same question could be asked by anyone regarding the industry they work in, the subject they're studying or the sport they're playing. Matt Finnigan offers the following advice:

"To find your niche, follow your passion. One of the reasons you may be interested in sports betting is a passion for a particular sport or watching sport in general. Your starting point should be the sport you know most about. Once identified, you need to break it down into a number of factors so that you can see how much you truly understand about the sport, and how much you need to learn. This will produce your blueprint for betting on it – both the sport in general, and the various markets that are available for doing so."

Use the activity below to help you to assess where your sweet spot might be.

Activity: finding your sweet spot

Take some time to reflect on your trading and answer the following questions:

Betting strengths
What do you feel are your natural talents and strengths when it comes to sports betting?

Betting/sporting interests
What sports and markets are you naturally interested in?
Which sports and markets have you bet on recently?

Motivation
What are you most passionate about?
Which sports do you enjoy researching and finding out more about?

Performance
What do you feel you can be best at? What markets have you traded? Which do you understand the most?
Do the markets have sufficient liquidity to enable you to achieve your goals?
Is there an area where you have a specific edge – access to knowledge or software?

Results
Where have your best results come from?
Where do you feel you could be most profitable?

What did you notice?
Are you currently acting in line with your findings? Where? Where not?
How could you utilise your strengths, interests, skills and talents more effectively?

Warming up – PREParation

"Winning is the science of being prepared"

– George Allen, Sr.

Review: current betting preparation reflection

What do you do to prepare before you bet?

Take a moment to list your preparation routine.

....

....

....

....

....

Are you consistent with this? If not, when do you do your preparation and when don't you?

What do average sports bettors and average sportspeople have in common?

They both generally spend less time and energy on *preparing* to perform than successful bettors and athletes. You only need to see the casual gym goer perform their quick leg shake and arm jiggle to know that all they really want to do is get on some machine and start 'exercising', just as in the same way the average bettor wants to get a bet on as quickly as possible with as little preparation and planning. In both cases, accident – a pulled muscle, a betting loss – is never far behind.

Quick – I need to get a bet on

"Spend anything more than a matter of minutes in a betting shop environment and you will notice that the majority of punters are betting not because they have studied the form and have unearthed a horse that fits their selection criteria. They are betting because the next race is about to start and are hastily scampering to the counter to get their slip through the scanner before the stalls open. They are not making considered rational choices and are not likely to be successful."

– Bruce Millington, in
The Definitive Guide to Betting on Sports

Becoming successful at sports betting will involve you adopting performance habits that most other people will get bored with or feel uncomfortable doing. Preparation is a key component of the performance cycle, is what keeps you in a feedback loop that is essential to continual improvement and goal achievement).

The performance cycle

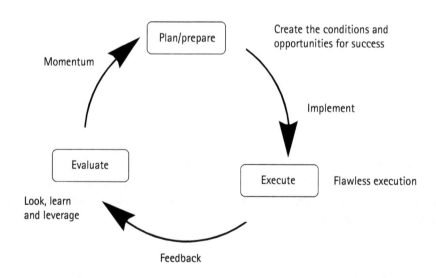

Being prepared for your betting is critical if you want consistency.

> ### Laziness leads to the poorhouse
>
> "All losing punters are lazy and will place a bet with little or no research beforehand. Again, this can be linked to being conditioned to lose: they view having a bet as a way merely to enhance enjoyment of watching live sport, and their efforts (and consequent successes) are commensurate with this. In the long term, there will be little entertaining about all that money wasted.
>
> "Do your research. Laziness leads to the poorhouse. You won't make money if you don't do your homework."
>
> – Matt Finnigan

Why prepare?

"Before everything else, getting ready is the secret of success."

– Henry Ford

Let's look firstly at some of the benefits of being prepared before you bet, and then secondly at the components of what may be included within a pre-betting warm-up routine.

What are the benefits of preparation?

- Consistency – repeating the same process each time before you bet provides you with an opportunity to establish some consistency of behaviour and performance.

- Confidence – knowing that you have prepared can give you a real confidence boost – and knowing that you have not prepared or have under prepared can certainly give you an uneasy feeling.

- Control – preparation is a part of the betting day over which you have full control. What you prepare and how well you do it is entirely down to you.

- Composure – If you have prepared fully and considered some 'what if' scenarios, then one big edge that you now have is that, should those events occur, your level of preparedness will enhance your ability to act quickly and calmly.

- Concentration – your preparation routine becomes a trigger to activate a focused trading mindset and transition you from waking or working mode.

- Reduced risk – being prepared reduces the risk of missing out on key information, making mistakes and errors and making bets that were born from a poor decision-making process.

The general rule for betting well is to do as much preparation as you know you need. Never skimp.

Below is a tried-and-tested framework that you can use as a starting point for developing your own preparation.

 Put it into practice – P.R.E.P.

1. Plan and prepare

- Research and analysis for upcoming sporting event.

- Read through your betting strategy and work out your strategy for betting/trading, including your risk management.

"Research is the key. You are taking on the odds compilers at the bookies and going head to head with other punters on the exchanges. Knowing the sport, the players, the history and any other fact which may affect the outcome of the event can help to give you a significant head start."

– Peter Webb

2. Rehearse

- Imagine yourself placing your bets, and also imagine some 'what ifs' happening and how you will deal with them if they do occur (see below). This is a mental run-through of what might happen and is a great way to 'test' your strategy in advance and to pre-programme some responses you might need to make.

---

3. Eventualities

- Consider 'what ifs' from your strategy and what you will do if those situations arise. This is a very important step. Prepare for adversity, for dealing with difficult market conditions.

"You think you know what is going to happen when you do your research and analysis and you will trade the game accordingly. Yet you also have to plan all your 'what if' options. If the team you have laid goes ahead, will you trade out and accept a loss? Will you lay them again at a better price? Will you stay in the trade and hope they concede, but have a stop loss in mind where you will definitely trade out? You need to have a trading plan for every outcome."

– Steve Taylor

4. Positive state

- Check you are in a positive state before you start betting – use a simple 0-10 scale (0 = very poor state, 10 = ideal state). If you are low on the scale, consider not betting. Your mental and physical state has a big impact on your alertness, reaction time, decision making and discipline.

Taking action

Now you have read this section, take time to write down a few notes about what you feel are the key points. Next, consider how they apply to you in your own sports betting. Finally, think about how you can take action.

Notes

How does this apply to me?

How can I take action?

4 Keep Score

"Feedback is the breakfast of champions."

– Ken Blanchard and Spencer Johnson

In this chapter:

- The benefits of record keeping and evaluation
- Keeping a written record of your bets
- Evaluating your betting

The benefits of record keeping and evaluation

Keeping written records and evaluating your betting performance is a key part of adopting a professional approach and is critical to achieving your full betting and profit potential. Evaluation is a part of the continual improvement process of the performance cycle and of adopting a mastery approach.

You should be continually seeking to maximise the effectiveness of your strategy. This process should involve continual re-examination of your records to identify whether elements of your system can be improved upon. From these records you can analyse trends and see where you are most and least successful and amend your strategy accordingly.

Without written records it is very difficult for evaluation and analysis to occur. Without evaluation and analysis it is very difficult for performance improvement to occur.

The vast majority of people in sports betting have no written record of their bets and do little evaluation or analysis of their results; the small proportion of people who do, tend to be those who are winning or improving.

Why do people not keep records and fail to undertake sufficient evaluation and analysis?

1. They choose not to – they do not want to allocate the time and effort to this area of betting, most likely because their betting is for entertainment and fun, or because they cannot be bothered; they are lazy.

2. They are unaware of the real benefits and value to be had from doing so.

3. They do not know how to record and evaluate and analyse their data effectively.

4. They have processes in place but they are so complex and intricate that sustaining them becomes a challenge and using the expanses of data they have collected is not possible.

What was I playing at when I was not writing everything down?

"I have to admit that there was a time when I used to feel great discomfort upon hearing a punter preaching about the importance of keeping records. It was something I never did, through a fusion of laziness and a fear that if I had my recent betting history thrust before me in all its gory detail it would reveal that I was an even less successful punter than I suspected.

"Finally, though, after a particularly bleak spell, I took on board one of the most basic rules a sensible punter imposes on himself and began chronicling all my bets. I now wonder what I was playing at when I was not writing everything down. Examination of betting records may sound like a boring, and sometimes painful, task but it is nothing of the sort. To be able to pinpoint where you are prospering and where you are bleeding money is crucial to your future success. You can use your records to analyse precisely which types of bets are coming off and which are costing you money. Being a good punter is mainly about knowing which potential avenues of profit are turning into financial dead ends. You can only truly work this out by keeping strict records and studying them at regular intervals."

– Bruce Millington in
The Definitive Guide to Betting on Sports

Interestingly, one of the most common barriers that people find in the way of keeping logs, or evaluating their betting, is the time it takes. There's some truth to this, but not enough that you should let it prevent you from doing so. Evaluation does not have to be massively time consuming, particularly with the help of spreadsheets and computers. And it is better by far to think of the time it still takes as a *time investment*. Time spent recording and evaluating is an investment in that it helps to develop and improve performance, and therefore results. It tells you in numerical terms how you are *actually* performing, which can be different to how you think you are doing. It can help you to identify patterns, both useful and limiting, in your betting, which if acted upon will impact on your profitability.

Keeping a written record of your bets

"How many punters have a record of every bet they have made?"

– Bill Esdaile

Keeping a written record of your bets is essential if you are going to perform any kind of useful evaluation of your performance.

What did you have to eat for lunch six weeks ago last Tuesday? Can you remember? Probably not.

What did you eat the last time you went out for a really great meal?

Can you remember? Probably!

Why is this?

When you had your lunch six weeks ago last Tuesday the chances are that this was a typical weekday lunch – probably a part of your daily routine, not overly exciting, and therefore not that memorable. When you recall your last great meal out, it is likely that it was more unique and had a greater emotional intensity to it.

Your memory is coded largely by the strength of the emotional attachment to that memory. Strong emotion (positive or negative) equals strong memory coding. Weak emotional intensity equals weaker memory coding.

In betting terms, you are going to remember bets that are big winners or losers, or are out of the ordinary, unique, in other ways – *but these are probably the minority of your bets*. Your day-to-day bets, which will form the bulk of your betting and which will determine, over time, your overall success, will not be remembered. A whole wealth of information in that data is therefore lost.

Your results and performance measures are a reflection of your betting behaviour – they will leave many clues as to what you have done well and where you can improve. Most importantly, they are objective – the numbers are the numbers, and are less prone to the psychological biases that interfere with our subjective evaluations.

It's time to stop betting on darts

"The only reason I stopped betting on darts was because one day I took the time to look at all of my betting results on a spreadsheet. And I noticed this whole lot of losses. When I took a closer look they all came from darts. I actually thought I had been doing okay, but the spreadsheet told the truth."

– Tony Hargraves

How good are you?

Rate yourself on the following attributes on a 1-10 scale, where 10 is high and 1 is low.

Driving ability ......

Work performance ......

Intelligence ......

Physical looks ......

What did you give yourself?

It is common for most people to rate themselves as average or above (scoring 5 or higher in each category), skewing the results to average or better. But obviously, assuming a normal distribution, in actual fact some people would be at the lower end, some at the higher, and the bulk in the middle.

Research in the field of behavioural finance shows people are prone to overestimating their abilities in their fiscal activities quite as much as in any other department of life.

"People who say 'I am a small winner' are probably losing money."

– Compton Hellyer

What should we record?

'How is your betting going?'

When you are asked that question, what is your reply, and on what evidence/data is that reply based? Whether you answer 'all right', 'good', 'okay', 'great' or 'not so well', I would hazard a guess that for most of you, as is the case with most people that bet on sports, the key driver behind your analysis of your performance is how much money you have made or lost recently. But, whilst the amount of money you are making or losing is the obvious measure of your performance and is definitely one to watch, it is not the most accurate or important measure.

In sport it is possible for a team to play well and lose, and for a team to play badly and win. In betting this is also true. You can be betting well – researching, planning, managing risk, being rational – and lose. And likewise you can bet badly – emotionally, with no risk management, no research – and win. If you measured your success purely on the outcome of your bet, then you could potentially feel bad when you bet well and feel great when you bet badly. There is a huge danger in this. You begin to associate negative feelings with the process of betting well and positive feelings with the process of betting badly. Over time your brain will drive you towards the behaviours where it gets the most rewards. You are conditioning yourself to undertake ill-disciplined betting.

A second 'danger' in using money made or lost as your only performance measure is that it does not take into account the two key components in the betting equation – you and the markets you have been betting on. Market/event conditions can be recorded simply and objectively in your betting records: in terms of the amount of liquidity, the range of prices traded, and then, more subjectively, in terms of your view of market movements and what happened to prices during an event.

Thirdly, when you use money as your sole or primary performance measure it is easy to get caught in the trap of making your confidence and sense of self-worth depend on your financial results. This can be an underlying cause of the emotional rollercoaster that many people experience. *Your betting results are not you.* They are the outcome of your performance and your behaviours within prevailing market events.

Interestingly, too strong a focus on outcome is one of the biggest causes of performance anxiety in sport and performance. It's the same for betting, and is partly why too strong a focus on money prevents many people from achieving their best possible results.

Measuring more than just money

Apart from your financial results, what other aspects of your betting performance can be measured that might prove useful?

What feedback can you get about how well you are betting, other than how much you are winning or losing?

There are three key categories of measure:

- outcome

- performance

- process.

We have already dealt with outcome. When we consider the result of a bet or betting period, this is what we are looking at. It is the simplest way to measure performance, and is often the most widely used. And yet, as we have seen, it is not necessarily the most useful in terms of improving performance.

After outcome, we can look at performance measures.

If you didn't ever get to see your betting bank or betting results, how would you know how well you were doing? How could you measure your performance other than by monetary results?

Here is the result of a football game: *Manchester United 1 – 1 Chelsea.*

What does that tell us? Well, that it was a draw; that United scored one goal and that Chelsea scored one; and that Manchester United were at home. Is the result, the score, an absolute measure of the performance of the teams?

If we wanted to really find out more about that game, wouldn't it be great to know how many shots on goal each team had; how much possession they had; the number of corners won by each side; whether a full-strength team was fielded by both or not; the number of free kicks conceded/awarded; the passing success rate; the referee's decisions; etc. In golf (greens in regulation, putts per round, holes parred, handicaps), tennis (winners, forced errors, percentage of first serves in) and Formula 1 (telemetry), metrics are widely used to assess and improve performance. When we get access to these performance measures, we can get a much clearer picture of what happened in a sporting event.

Importantly for the individuals and teams, by looking at such statistics they can and do look at ways to improve their performances. (And, as a bettor, you'll appreciate this as they are doubtlessly also things that you have looked at when assessing teams or individuals for your forthcoming bets.)

In the same way, the use of betting performance metrics helps us to get a clearer idea of how our betting results are created. The advantage of looking at performance metrics is that our ability to alter future performance is then put far more under our own control. What measures can you utilise in your betting to get a clearer picture of how you are betting?

Example betting performance metrics

- Number of bets placed
- Number and/or percentage of winners/losers
- Average winner (monetary amount)
- Average loser (monetary amount)
- Average winner/average loser (this is called the pay-off ratio)
- Number of backs vs. number lays
- Expectancy (% of winners x average winner) - (% of losers x average loser)

You could further categorise these by sport, and by market, to show you where you are making or losing the most money.

What else can we measure? Well, at the opposite end of the outcome is the aforementioned *process*.

What is covered in process? In sport it would include the application of tactics, maintaining positive psychology, nutritional strategies, warming up and cooling down, focus on performance of particular skills, and so on. In betting, this would cover aspects such as preparation and planning, bet selection, decision-making evaluation, and emotional state control.

Process goals are the most controllable aspect of our performance, and the least widely used or considered in betting. Identifying what the key processes of betting proficiently are, and then monitoring and measuring them, is an excellent way of improving performance over time.

Sample betting process measures

- Planning and preparation
- Bet selection/trading and decision-making
- Risk management/staking system and application to bets
- Mental state/emotional control (focus, confidence, patience, discipline)
- Evaluation

Process measures/actions are directly under our control, easier to improve on, and ultimately determine how well we bet.

Process measures can be difficult to assess as they are often less tangible in nature. One way of evaluating your process is to list the key ones and then to rate each on a 1-5 scale where 5 is it was done as well as possible and 1 is it was not done at all. This allows you to add some element of objectivity to the evaluation and to record and monitor your performance over time. I often challenge people who I coach to focus on developing and improving their process scores rather than focussing on their monetary returns and guess what happens? They achieve improved monetary returns as a result.

Example of process measures for betting on a sports event

Area	Score/5
Research and planning	4
'What if' scenarios	5
Trading strategy selection	4
Bet execution	4
Risk management/staking system followed	5
Emotional state	3
Post-event analysis	5
Total Score	30/35 (86%)

Another useful method can be to write a narrative description of your approach to betting that day, focusing on what you did, your actions and decisions.

Stepping slightly back from this, the final part of evaluating your process is to look at it in total and in terms of discipline. Ultimately there are four key components in terms of process to any bet you have.

	Win	Loss
Disciplined	1	2
Not disciplined	3	4

1. You are very disciplined, make a rational decision, manage risk and the bet is a winner.

2. As for 1, but the bet is a loser.

3. You take a random punt with no reasoning or plan and the bet wins.

4. As for 3, and the bet loses.

It is useful to finally evaluate your decision-making by categorising each bet according to the quadrants above. If you can reduce the numbers of 3s and 4s, and your strategy has an edge, then you *will* make more money over time.

* * *

Having a combination of outcome, performance and process measures will give you the best possible picture of how you are actually performing.

There is a great phrase that says 'What gets measured gets done'. Once you begin to measure your performance you will naturally want to improve it, and the beauty of performance and process measures is that they are more under your control and therefore easier to improve.

Getting the most from your records

There are some key considerations to be made to help you to get the most from your betting records.

1. Electronic or paper?

Some people like to have their logs and journals kept electronically and others like to keep theirs on paper, often in an A4 diary. The choice is purely down to the individual but a few points to bear in mind are:

- Accessibility – how easy is it to get to and see the data you want?

- Time – how long does inputting/writing take?

- Analysis – how easy is it to analyse the data you have?

2. Numbers or words?

When it comes to performance measures, keeping numerical data is very helpful. Numbers are objective and they are also easy to work with for the purposes of analysis and comparison, graphing/charting and visual representation.

However, the subjective side of our performance is equally important – what we felt during the bet, the reasoning behind our actions, etc., – that it is important to have some method for capturing these thoughts, too. My recommendation is to devise a system that enables you to record and track key numerical data and allows you to provide a subjective report of your performance alongside this. A spreadsheet and a diary is an ideal combination.

3. Complex or simple?

What I have discovered over my time working with people is that any record-keeping system is only as good as the data in it. One of the key aspects of a successful log is that it is always used and therefore boasts a large quantity of data. So the answer to complex vs. simple comes down to usability.

You could have the most amazingly complex and interesting records, but if filling them in takes a massive amount of your time and you end up either shortcutting or not undertaking the process at all, then the brilliance of their scheme is irrelevant.

Likewise, a process that is too simplistic, although kept everyday, may not have sufficient depth or quality of data to give it any significant value. And, ultimately, if there is little value coming from the process, you will soon stop doing it.

So aim for a recording method that is a blend of the complex and the useful, and that is not too time-consuming or time-constraining to put together. Exactly what this means, of course, will depend on personal circumstances and choices, but it should be achievable by just finding what works for you, and not being afraid to adjust if problems are creeping in.

4. How often should I log bets?

Every bet should be logged, as every bet tells some kind of story. Why, when and how you took the bet; why, when and how you got out; the size of your bet and what you learnt from that experience, are all very useful pieces of data. If you are selective in your logging of bets (e.g. only logging your winners) then your analysis will be skewed and will not be that useful. It will not reflect your whole betting picture. Avoiding logging your losing bets or the ill-disciplined ones is denial.

5. What should I record for each bet?

There are many things that you can log and evaluate. You may wish to consider as essentials:

1. Basic information – day, date, time.

2. Bet information – sport, market, bet size, reasons for placing the bet.

3. Summative evaluation of the bet, noting win/loss and any feedback – positives or negatives and points of learning; and also any market or event-specific information.

Put it into practice: keep betting records

Use the guidelines above to help you to develop your own log and perhaps an overall evaluation sheet for a periodic review – weekly or monthly.

Evaluating your betting

Looking back and reviewing your betting performance over a period of time is a fundamental part of the performance cycle. This process can take place in different forms over different time frames, including a day, a week, a month, a quarter, or the whole betting year.

In general, with people who are more active in their betting, a monthly review is standard, with a more in-depth one undertaken alongside it either quarterly or annually.

Looking at your betting data over a longer period will give you a greater sample size and greater reliability for analysing your betting. Conducting a longer-term review is something that I urge everyone to do. As well as being key, as we have seen, to correcting errors in one's betting and seeing accurately how one is performing, it is critical for developing your goals and objectives for the following betting period.

Below is a simple format that you can use to conduct a betting evaluation review. Once you have conducted the review, the most important step is to generate your goals and outcomes for the upcoming betting period and create some forward momentum.

 Put it into practice: conducting a periodic betting review

Look over your betting records for the period and collate them.

Now look over the data; calculate and evaluate:

- Gross profits/losses over the period (how much money you made or lost)
- Net profits/losses over the period (how much money have you made after all your costs, e.g. software, commissions, subscriptions for analysis)
- Number of bets placed
- Number of, and percentage (success rate) of winners: losers
- Biggest winner/loser

- Average winner/loser (pay-off ratio)
- Consecutive winners and losers
- Biggest period of drawdown/downswing
- Expectancy over that time

Look over the summary of your betting records and analyse the data – what story does it tell? It can also be useful here to cross-reference them against historical data.

How do your results look across different sports or markets?

....

What were your key achievements (performance and results)?

....

What evidence of progress is there?

....

What did you do well?

....

Where can you improve?

....

What are your key trading goals, objectives and actions for the next period?

....

Consider:

–   What should you continue to do?

–   What should you do more of?

–   What should you do less of?

–   What should you start doing?

–   What should you stop doing?

What help/support/resources do you need to achieve those goals/objectives?

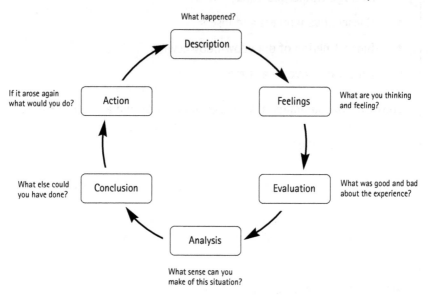

The Reflective Cycle

What happened?

Description

What are you thinking and feeling?

Feelings

If it arose again what would you do?

Action

What was good and bad about the experience?

Evaluation

What else could you have done?

Conclusion

Analysis

What sense can you make of this situation?

© Copyright High Performance Global Ltd

www.highperformanceglobal.com

Taking action

Now you have read this section, take time to write a few notes, detailing in particular the key points, then consider how they apply to you in your own sports betting, before finally thinking about how you can take action.

Notes

How does this apply to me?

How can I take action?

5 Make Rational Decisions

"How could I have been so stupid?"

– Sports bettors everywhere

In this chapter:

- Why rational decision-making matters
- How do you make a decision?
- What stops us being rational and what can we do about it?
- 10 ways to help you make more rational decisions

Why rational decision-making matters

"How could I have been so stupid?" This is a sentence (or a politer version of one with a similar meaning) that everyone who has been involved in sports betting in a regular way has yelled at some point.

You had a betting plan but you didn't follow it. You knew how much you were comfortable staking but you staked more. You knew that chasing losses was futile, but you still did it. You knew you shouldn't bet without doing your research but you did it anyway.

Betting is a series of decisions – what sport to bet on, what market to bet in, what strategy to apply, what stakes to use. And your betting results are an outcome of the decisions that you make. The more rational and more disciplined these decisions are, the more likely that the results you get will be positive.

This chapter will look at the important process of rational decision-making; it will also bring together some of the insights we've already seen in other areas of the book, and look at how they can be harnessed to this end.

How do you make a decision?

The United States Navy Fighter Weapons School is based at Naval Air Station Miramar in California. Many of you will know it best as the *Top Gun* school, where the US Navy's best pilots are brought for advanced training. The capabilities of what makes one fighter pilot better than another were studied by Capt John Boyd, a leading instructor and millitary strategist. His insights led him to develop a model for showing how the best pilots think. The model is known as OODA (Observe Orient Decide Act) and is highly applicable to decision-making in numerous activities – betting included.

It is relevant because any description of human behaviour in a strategic setting should include the processes it involves. Namely: developing *situational awareness, making decisions, and then acting in accordance with a set of desired outcomes.*

Below is a simplified version of the model with specific reference to sports betting (the full OODA model can be found in the appendix).

Simplified **OODA** model

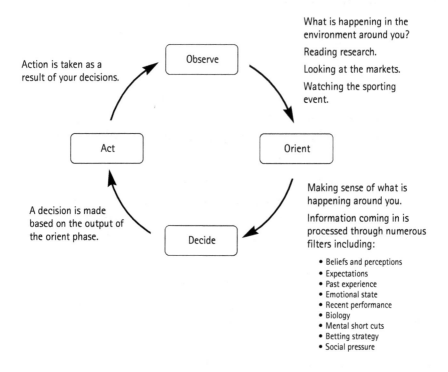

The first stage of the cycle is the *observation phase*, looking around and taking in information (visual or verbal).

The next is making sense of it in the *orient phase* – which, due to powerful unconscious processes, can happen in microseconds; or, in a longer loop, can be done very consciously and analytically.

This then outputs a *decision.*

And, finally, the opportunity to *act.*

This loop is continually running. The most important part of the model to understand in relation to making rational betting decisions is the orient phase. It is here that the information that you are taking in, which we could say is neutral (it is what it is), is interpreted and given meaning by you. This is the precursor to any decisions and actions you take. What happens in the orient phase generates rational and disciplined decisions or irrational and ill-disciplined ones. It is where professional or unprofessional bets are determined and born.

What stops us from being rational and what can we do about it?

> *"Short-term self-protection, ignorance, excitement and biases are the root of most failures of judgement. We believe that by identifying the psychological causes behind many types of financial decisions, you can effectively change your behaviour in ways that will ultimately put more money in your pocket and help you keep more of what you already have."*
>
> – *Why Smart People Make Big Money Mistakes*, Gary Belsky and Thomas Gilovich
> (Simon & Schuster, 2000)

Studying financial decision-making and the factors that influence it has become a recognised academic discipline known as 'behavioural economics' or 'behavioural finance'. One way of making more rational, and therefore profitable, betting decisions is to have a greater understanding of why people make irrational decisions and to know what you can do about it – to have strategies to maximise your rationality and your profitability. Warren Buffett, the world's most successful investor, suggests that one of the keys to successful decision making is avoiding "the temptations and urges that get people in to trouble". This is very true in sports betting.

Some of the key things that are involved in the orient phase, and that can be the site of issues leading to ill-disciplined sports betting, are motivations; beliefs and perceptions; mental and emotional states.

Motivations

Your motivations are a key driver of your behaviour. The brain has a natural goal-seeking mechanism and will go after what you programme it for. If you are betting for excitement and fun and for an adrenaline rush, for example, then the resulting decisions and actions will be very different to what you would get if you were betting with profits and professionalism in mind.

Being aware of your motivations for betting and understanding the effects of these motivations on your behaviour are key. A professional approach focused on making profits over time will give you the greatest chance of success in the long run.

See: chapter 2, 'Bet for Profits, Not Excitement', page 21.

Are you looking for fun or value?

"I have seen so many people get sucked into the 'fun bet' markets as opposed to looking for where there is real value."

– Ian Massie

Beliefs and perceptions

"Get your facts first and then you can distort them as much as you like."

– Mark Twain

You see what you want to see. When you are looking at research and watching the markets and sporting events you need to try and do so with as much of an open and objective mind as is possible. This is the best way of avoiding confirmation bias, which is where your mind seeks to reinforce views and opinions, beliefs and perceptions, that you already hold.

If you start by believing that a particular team have an exceptionally good chance of beating another, then you will unconsciously begin to look for evidence that supports your case. Meanwhile you will unknowingly also discount any evidence that may be contrary to it. This is why in science it is important to attempt to disprove a theory as much as to prove it; it is the only way to neutralise such naturally occurring and largely unconscious thinking. A good phrase to keep in mind is 'I'll see it when I believe it.'

Your beliefs and perceptions are an overlay on top of the reality of what is happening in the betting markets. You are in fact never actually betting on those markets. You are betting on your beliefs and perceptions about them. Help to manage confirmation bias by always asking yourself 'What else is happening?', 'What am I missing?' or 'Could I be wrong?'

See: Chapter 1, 'Think Differently', page 1.

See: Chapter 1, 'Think Differently', page 1.

┌─ Clouding your view ─────────────────────────────────┐

"Punters often have a lack of price sensitivity; they get carried away; it clouds their view."

– Ian Massie

└──┘

Mental and emotional states

How you feel has a big impact on how you orient and the decisions you make. Ever been to the supermarket when you are feeling hungry? What happened? If you're like most people, you probably bought more food and of a less nutritious nature than usual. Your shopping behaviour was driven by your dominant feeling at the time – hunger. Here are some emotional states that, if experienced, can lead to decisions and actions that are not conducive to profitable sports betting.

Boredom

There can be periods where not much is happening and the markets you bet on are quiet. The danger here is that you get bored and bet merely to do something, rather than because a betting opportunity as defined by your strategy has arisen. Ask yourself – are you betting to relieve boredom or to make money? The same goes for when it isn't quiet, but you cannot identify any bets which truly comply with your proven strategies. Find other things to do in situations like this – reading, research, strategy development. It doesn't mean that you can't be involved in betting activity, simply that the activity itself ought not to be betting.

Fatigue and mental overload, leading to poor concentration

Betting can involve long or unsociable hours sometimes, not least because many people are betting as well as holding down full-time jobs. As you begin to tire, your risk of error is greatly increased (hence the tight working hours' controls placed on people in safety-critical environments). And your performance levels *will* decline. Manage your physical energy levels by ensuring that you get good quality sleep, stay hydrated and do not go hungry and avoid betting when you are already feeling tired.

Anger and frustration

The changes that occur to your physiology and psychology when you are angry and frustrated affect your ability to make objective and reasoned decisions. You are greatly at risk when trading emotionally and not objectively. Take a time-out and wait until you are in a good trading state before betting again.

Overconfidence

Overconfidence is a dangerous feeling – it can get you involved in betting with bigger stakes than are appropriate. Create awareness of when overconfidence might occur for you. Be alert for such situations. And, where necessary, stop betting.

Greed

Wanting too much too soon, or trying to make every bet a big winner, are common errors. Taking a long-term and risk-management-oriented perspective is key at all times.

Fear

This can come in many forms, the main ones being fear of loss and fear of missing out. This can lead to you not taking bets that are actually a part of your strategy. Managing your staking, accepting losses as a part of betting, and having confidence in your betting strategy and your own betting ability will all help to reduce or eliminate any fears. If you have the right approach and mindset in place, there is no cause for trepidation because you know that losses are inevitable – but so are bigger and more frequent wins *over time*.

Being aware of emotional states that impact negatively on your betting and aiming to avoid them as much as possible, spending as much time in positive states as you can, and then managing them when they do occur, helps significantly in making more effective decisions and being more disciplined.

See: 'Dealing with performance-limiting emotions positively', page 129.

Don't back your own team!

"One way of keeping some emotion out of your betting is to not bet on your own team – a common mistake that is made by the casual punter."

– Wally Pyrah

"Never bet on anything to which you have an emotional attachment. If your favourite football team are playing, then get your buzz from watching them play, and not from betting on them."

– Tony Hargraves

Past experience and current performance

What has happened to us in the past, both recent and distant, can affect our decisions in the present. We are very driven by pain and pleasure – always seeking to move away from pain and towards pleasure – and this can be a big driver of our behaviours. We seek to avoid making decisions or taking actions that led to pain in the past, whilst striving to take those that have led to feelings of pleasure. The challenge here is that, as we have discussed, it is possible to take the correct actions and lose money, and make poor decisions and make money. So if we are attaching pain and pleasure to making or losing money then we can in fact be driving ourselves towards decisions and behaviours that are not disciplined.

It is important to see each bet as a new bet, to see each event as being independent of the past. It should be thought of like flipping a series of coins; the outcome of each flip is entirely separate from the previous one, no matter how much we sometimes like to think it isn't. You need to be able to execute your betting strategy knowing that the right decision is the right decision irrespective of what has occurred or how you are feeling as a result.

How much time you have to make the decision

The time frame that you have to make a decision plays a big part in the final outcome. When there is a 'long' period of time you are able to enter into a far more rational decision-making process – one that is more conscious, effortful, explicit and logical. This is what you should enjoy when planning and researching a betting opportunity prior to an event starting.

A rational decision-making process

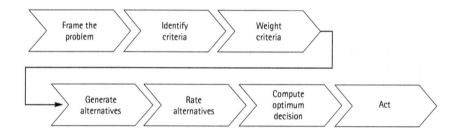

Where time is much shorter – for example, when you are betting in-running in a fast-moving market – it is not possible to go through those seven steps. Instead, you utilise a quicker but more primitive thinking process (often referred to as 'System 1' thinking, but don't get hung up on terminology). It is used to help you to make decisions in fast-paced, pressurised and uncertain circumstances. It is a faster, more intuitive, automatic, effortless, implicit and often emotional process. But it leaves you far more prone to making irrational decisions and errors, since your brain has to take shortcuts to enable such decision and action to occur.

Nevertheless, since we have to rely on it in at least one stage of our betting (the action), it is good to know that it can be harnessed and improved.

Intuition and cognition

Let's consider cricket. A batsman is facing a fast bowler, who bowls a bouncer at 80 mph. The batsman has a split second to assess and take action. He must comprehend numerous variables, including the speed and movement of the ball, the speed and direction of the wind, the likely place and pace of the bounce on the pitch, the quality of the pitch in that area and what it might impart to the ball's movement, the placement of the field – all faster than can be verbalised. Expert performers in situations of such uncertainty often have no time for calm, rational decision making. But they prevail. The process has become subconscious – what we sometimes call *intuitive*.

The process of being able to make these successful intuitive decisions is learnt. It is called implicit learning. Patterns are internalised and decisions made in response to them over tens of thousands of trials.

When you have been exposed to thousands of examples of betting prices, markets and events, your subconscious mind is able to extract patterns from them to enable an efficient subconscious, System 1, decision-making process. This is what you may call gut feeling or intuition. It is important to stress that the reliability of your gut feeling is dependent on your exposure to the markets, and that there is a big difference between 'intuition' and 'intuwishing'.

Practice makes perfect, runs the cliché. But it's psychologically as well as proverbially true.

 For an interesting read on the impact of intuition and subconscious decision-making, read Malcolm Gladwell's book *Blink*.

Biology

Belsky and Gilovich, in their book *Why Smart People Make Big Money Mistakes*, state that expecting mechanical precision from human beings is foolish. Attempting to override millennia of programming is a major challenge. The abilities to compute moving averages, build spacecraft and understand cricket are relatively recent and sophisticated biological innovations.

We can't afford to underestimate the power of the inner primate whose primary need was survival and not, alas, making money from betting on sport. Sports betting can drive us to do things that make no logical sense – but make perfect emotional sense. In some ways, as Jason Zweig states in *Your Money and Your Brain*, "[t]hat does not make us irrational. It makes us human. Our brains were originally designed to get more out of whatever would improve our odds of survival and to avoid what would worsen the odds." Many of our human instincts are emotionally driven and are contrary to the analytical processes needed to be successful in something like sports betting. Learning to think and act in rational ways, utilising our more recently developed 'smart brain', is a key part of the learning and development process for achieving success. It is something this book has tried, in effect, to address continually.

How your brain processes making and losing money

In his book, *Your Money and Your Brain*, Jason Zweig cites neuroscientific research that suggests that when you lose money the same part of your brain is activated as that which deals with mortal danger. Likewise, when you make money you activate parts of the brain that are activated in a similar way by the consumption of morphine or cocaine.

Your betting strategy

Not having a clearly defined strategy with an edge is a big problem. It makes it very difficult to make a disciplined decision, as there is no legitimate framework or guidelines for what and when to undertake specific behaviours – or, indeed, when *not* to. And this leaves an open playing field for your mind to interpret and act in a hazardous and less structured way. Without having clearly defined betting opportunities you will be betting in little better than a random fashion. Having a clearly defined betting strategy provides the framework and filters for making better quality and more disciplined decisions.

There are numerous resources out there on devising winning sports-betting strategies – more, indeed, than there are on executing such strategies flawlessly (hence this book) – and it is always worth studying and adapting them to keep on top of this problem. Remember what we said earlier: the holy grail of betting (what works for you), will have to be repeatedly pursued in the face of changing markets. So commit to excellence and take a real interest in the art of betting strategies.

See: 'Hitting the sweet spot', page 44.

Preparation

Preparation is something we looked at in detail in chapter 3. If you are unprepared when you start betting, then any events that occur will force you into being reactive, and more emotionally driven. By preparing, doing your research, and looking at 'what if' scenarios, you can create a mental framework that enables you to be proactive in your approach. And when you have to be reactive, having already considered the situations where it's likely to be necessary, you'll be forearmed and able to act more effectively.

In terms of preparation and research, it is interesting to note that all the people I interviewed for the book stressed the importance of using statistics and hard data as a part of that process, so as to make it more rational and objective – and ultimately much more helpful.

See: 'Warming up - PREParation', page 47.

Mental shortcuts – biases

"The brain seeks to make decisions in the easiest way possible, with the least possible emotional cost and the least mental effort (cognitive cost)."

– Jason Zweig, *Your Money and Your Brain* (Souvenir Press, 2005)

As a part of the decision-making process, the brain can utilise a number of biases (shortcuts) in order to make the process simpler and quicker. However, not *necessarily* more rational or profitable. That requires something extra.

Simple puzzle

The bat and ball together cost £1.10. The bat costs £1.00 more than the ball. How much does the ball cost?

Almost everyone at first glance says 10p. Most people will not notice that they are wrong unless they are asked to look again, and given more time to do so. Initially your brain looked for what was most obvious, and felt right – it took a shortcut – and only with more time and conscious analytical processing is the right answer eventually arrived at.

If the ball is 10p and the bat is £1.00 more, then the bat is £1.10 – and that plus the ball at 10p gives a total of £1.20. The correct answer is that the ball is 5p, making the bat £1.05 and giving a total of £1.10.

Representation bias

Read the phrases in the triangles below.

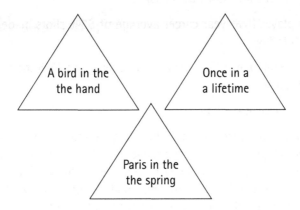

Now read them again slowly. Did you spot the 'the the' (twice) and the 'a a'?

The representativeness bias is related to stereotyping and generalising and how these are used as shortcuts to forming beliefs and making a decision about things. We tend to imagine that what we see, or expect to see, is typical of what should and will occur. We are often unaware of the possibility of unusual events happening. In sports betting, where uncertainty is high, it is important to think about what could happen and not just what should happen.

The law of small numbers

The law of small numbers states that it does not take long for people to jump to conclusions and to establish trends and patterns. In fact neuroscience has shown how our brain is pattern-seeking. Once an event has occurred twice, it is already starting to look unconsciously and uncontrollably for the third repetition.

People in sports betting can too often observe small samples and assume that all these samples represent the population as a whole. How many betting decisions have been made on seven or eight observations of the market, and are then assumed to be dependable? These observations may work in the short term, but are unlikely to give any long-term consistency. How much testing should you do? The standard in statistics is to have a minimum of 30 samples; however, you will probably want to have as big a sample size as is possible and realistic.

The hot hand phenomena

Imagine that you're the coach of a basketball team. There's 10 seconds left and your team is down by a basket.

Your star player (five-year career average of 55% shots made) is only two for 10 today.

Another veteran player (five-year career average of 45% shots made) is 10 for 10 today.

Whom do you give the ball to?

Whilst almost all sports fans, coaches, players and anyone else for that matter would give the ball to the player who has made ten shots from ten – that is the player with the hot hand – research by Thomas Gilovich and Amos Tversky (leaders in the field of behavioural fiance) demonstrated that this view does not hold up to scrutiny.

In their research they analysed the field goal records of four professional basketball teams and came to the inescapable conclusion that regardless of how many shots a player has made or missed in a row, the odds that he will make or miss his next shot are the same as you would expect from his overall, career-long shooting average. In our case above, a 55% career shooter is more likely to hit any given shot than a 45% career shooter *regardless* of their immediately previous short-term history and performances.

Emotionally it feels like it should be the guy with the 'hot hand' who is in form today – your veteran player. Statistically, however, the star player has a far greater shooting average over the biggest (five-year) sample size and so would be the rational choice.

Imagine flipping a coin. The chance of a coin coming up heads at any time is 50%. If you flip a coin 20 times in a row there is an 80% chance of three heads or three tails in a row, a 50% chance of four in a row and a 25% chance of a streak of five. But at any given point in the series, the odds of a head on the next flip will be 50%. Similarly, in basketball and in other sports, and more importantly in betting, there are bound to be streaks of random hits and misses, and of random wins and losses.

Situational pressures

Sometimes life events outside of betting can create pressures and stresses within it. Perhaps the most destructive of all situational pressures are financial ones, where your focus shifts to 'having to make money' and your betting approaches become more loose and more risky in order to meet your short-term financial need.

Other situational pressures include life events such as births, deaths, marriages, moving house, and changes in employment. Being aware of what is happening outside of your betting is important and having the discipline not to bet if you are distracted by external events is key.

Summary: 10 ways to help you to make more rational decisions

 Put it into practice: 10 ways to help you to make more rational decisions

1. Bet for profits and not for excitement.
2. Develop a betting strategy with an edge and commit to sticking to it.
3. Emphasise decisions over results and attach pain and pleasure to the process of betting, not the outcomes (the money).
4. Do your research and utilise statistics and mathematics as a part of formulating your betting decisions.
5. Don't bet on your own team.
6. Stay open minded and objective and be aware of any biases that may be affecting your thinking.
7. Treat every betting decision as unique and independent of every other.
8. Manage your risk.
9. Only bet when you are 'emotionally fit' to do so.
10. If life outside of betting is stressful and distracting then take a break.

Taking action

Now you have read this section, take time to write a few notes, the key points, then consider how they apply to you in your own sports betting, before finally thinking about how you can take action.

Notes

How does this apply to me?

How can I take action?

6 Don't Chase Losses

"Learn the hardest lesson first – and that is how to take losses."

– Tony Hargraves

In this chapter:

- Why do people chase losses?
- How to stop chasing losses

Jim was a successful sales manager. Every day he studied the racing form and came up with his best three bets of the day. His avowed intent was to have £100 on each of them. If any one (or more) of the three bets that he had spent several hours researching won, Jim would be satisfied, collect his winnings and retire for the day.

However, if all three bets lost, Jim began looking for other bets to get his money back on. He staked more and more on horses on which he had done little or no research. On some days he was able to recover his losses; on others he ended up losing several thousand pounds.

Jim was eventually declared bankrupt and lost his house.

* * *

Nobody likes to lose when they are betting, but if you are going to be successful at sports betting over time then you have to learn how to lose. The irony is that most people lose money trying to avoid losses. Earlier we looked at the importance of not being fixated on picking winners. This is the other, perhaps more difficult, side of that. You need to be able to take a loss and move on.

Words of wisdom

"NEVER chase your losses."

– Bill Esdaile

"Bookies love people who chase losses."

– Compton Hellyer

Why do people chase losses?

Read the scenarios below. Then, for each, choose either option A or B. Take the exercise as seriously as possible – as if you actually had the money in your hand.

Scenario 1

Imagine that you have just been given £1,000 and you have been asked to then choose between two options. With option A you are guaranteed to win an additional £500. With option B, you are given the chance to flip a coin. If it is heads, you win another £1,000; tails, you get nothing more. Which would you choose?

Scenario 2

Now imagine you have just been given £2,000 and are required to choose between two options. With option A you are guaranteed to lose £500. With option B you are given the chance to flip a coin. If it's heads you lose £1,000; tails you lose nothing. Which option would you choose?

* * *

How did you do? If you went for option A in the first one then you are with the majority of people who have been asked this question. You have taken the guaranteed additional £500 instead of taking the additional risk of flipping the coin and either winning £1,000 more or nothing.

❝ In a situation of gain most people become risk averse, whilst in a situation of loss they become risk seeking. ❞

If you went for option A in the second one then you would have been in the minority of people. You chose to guarantee your loss rather than to take the additional risk of flipping the coin, and either doubling that loss or avoiding it, which is the choice of the majority of people.

This exercise illustrates something very interesting. It has been conducted with a huge number of people and the results are nearly always along the same lines. It demonstrates that in a situation of gain most people become risk averse, whilst in a situation of loss they become risk seeking.

Chasing losses ────────────────────────────────

"I have seen the number of people who lose, how they lose, and how much they lose. I have seen the mistakes they make, like doubling their stakes when they have lost."

– Ian Massie

Is this doom and gloom for bettors, then? Are we condemned to chase our losses by a primordial psychological bias? No. Although it does mean that success for most people will take time and effort, it is something that we can train ourselves out of.

First we need to understand the basis for this problem.

Taking a loss is also not easy psychologically because:

- We don't like to lose. Many people are naturally competitive and most would rather not lose if given the choice. Keith Sobey's experience has shown him that "[m]any people have a competitive streak in their nature and hate to lose. Betting amplifies this tendency."

  ❝Are you betting to be right or to make money?❞

- Ego – your ego functions around the central premises of looking good and being right. Taking a loss can be seen as being wrong and is therefore a dent to ego. An important question to ask yourself is are you betting to be right or to make money?

You don't have to be right every time ────────────────────

"Most people think they know more than the market. In reality, the market does what it likes. I am there to find opportunities but I don't expect to be right every time."

– Peter Webb

Are you making matters worse?

Taking losses is not an instinctive or natural behaviour for most of us. It requires work and effort to master. It is interesting that many people compound this situation and make it even harder to do so because of how they approach their betting. Root this out and the battle is half won already.

1. Taking excessive risk in relation to your betting bank

When you take excessive risk in relation to your betting bank you are creating a higher level of mental stress for the duration of the bet. And you are setting yourself up for greater pain and anguish if you lose.

I like to encourage people to think about the relationship between the bets they place and the size of their betting banks, and to consider their betting bank size against their personal wealth. If your bets are a significant proportion of your betting bank then any given loss is also a big loss of your betting bank– a big double whammy. If your betting bank is also a large proportion of your personal wealth then you have a big triple whammy occurring, and that is not a pleasant experience for anyone.

It is important to consider your bet size in relation to the potential loss and to look at it from two key perspectives – the size of the financial loss, and the emotional pain of the loss. If either is too great (and often it can be both), then you are increasing your chances of succumbing to the urge to chase your losses.

Personal wealth, betting bank, bet-size relationship

Staking is key

"**Too many people have no consistent staking plan.**"

– Bill Esdaile

2. Not fully accepting of losses as a part of betting

As has been touched on before, at a deep level you have to internalise the fact that taking a loss is a natural part of betting and get to the level where the thought of a loss itself is not an issue for you. Everyone in betting loses.

Losses are inevitable

"**Over a period of time we cannot make profits without sustaining short-term losses.**"

– Matt Finnigan

3. Betting when you need to make money

Desperation is one of the most destructive states that you can be in when betting. When someone is desperate to make money, every betting opportunity becomes a good one. Risk management and staking plans go out of the window. Any loss is a significant one and the pain of taking it is too great. No matter how affordable, all of a sudden you cannot afford to take it; you bet on to try and recover it. And you very rarely succeed in this.

How to stop chasing losses

It is unlikely that you chase every loss you have. So what determines our reaction to a loss and whether we chase it or not?

In summary, it's:

- the size of the loss (financial and emotional pain)

- how good you felt your chances were of winning (frustration and disappointment)

- how you lost (a losing bet or a bad bet?)

- how your recent performance has been (the bigger picture – compounds or cushions your emotions)

- the size of your betting bank (secondary level of financial and emotional pain)

- the way you perceive and explain the loss to yourself (your psychological resilience).

 Review: reflection on losses

Think about a loss you have incurred recently – what was it about it that hurt?

Think about different losses, the factors that affected how you felt about that loss and your reaction to it.

Manage your risk

We've established already the importance of accepting losses. There are ways of making this mental adjustment easier. A key part of this is managing your risk.

Accepting a loss is significantly smoother if the financial amount of the loss is within your 'loss comfort zone'. If you have a bank of £1,000 and you lose £100 (10%), that is likely to be significantly more painful than if you lost £10 (1%). Losing £500 is going to sting.

When assessing how much you are willing to lose, you should consider two dimensions:

1. Financial – how much can you afford to lose? How much of that are you *willing* to lose?

2. Emotional – how much can you lose without being affected by it emotionally?

Aim to make your loss threshold fit within both of these parameters and you will find that your emotional and behavioural reaction to losses is drastically different.

Know when to take losses

For people who are betting in-play and trading sports spreads, one of the most important techniques to implement to help with your discipline in taking losses is to identify a point at which you will take the loss prior to putting the bet on. You are at your most rational when there is no bet on, and this level of rationality decreases the further you go in the process of making a bet. It also decreases the further your loss grows. It is very difficult to find a good place to take a loss once your bet is on. The answer *must* be sooner rather than later. Many of the most successful sports traders use 'stop losses' to manage their risk, identifying points in the market where they will take their loss in advance of placing the bet.

Have a loss ritual

What do you currently do following a loss?

a. Moan and groan and blame someone or something.

b. Get angry and shout.

c. Throw something.

d. Find something to bet on to recover the loss as quickly as possible.

e. All of the above.

When you have a losing bet it can help if you have a short ritual, a process you go through, that helps you to deal with the loss and then move on. Rituals are powerful because they help to change your thinking and state with, over time, minimal effort.

Put it into practice: a loss ritual

1. Stop – take a break; perhaps go for a walk.

2. Review – reflect on what happened and why.

3. Learn – what would you do differently next time?

4. Release – let go of the loss; once you have learnt from it, the value in it has gone.

5. Re-focus – get ready for the next bet.

Take a new perspective

Perspective is very powerful. How we choose to look at events can have a big impact on how we feel about them. Two useful perspectives that you can take to help to deal with adverse events more effectively are the 'wide lens' and the 'long lens'.

The wide lens encourages you to take a wider perspective to look at what you can take out of the event *other* than the result. The key question to ask to engage this perspective is 'What can I learn from this?'

A sense of perspective: Michael Jordan takes the wide lens

"I have missed more than 9,000 shots in my career. I have lost almost 300 games. On 26 occasions I have been entrusted to take the game-winning shot... and I missed. I have failed over and over and over again in my life. And that's precisely why I succeed."

– Michael Jordan

There are lessons in every loss, setback or error – they are learning opportunities. If there has been a financial loss then this can be seen as a cost of learning, and can then be 'invested' in making future returns by not repeating the mistake or error. This is taking a wide lens view.

"Learn from your mistakes and losses – you cannot win every time."

– Steve Taylor

"Losing money hurts. I don't look at it as losing money but as a step to making money in the long run. When I was a young guy I was in sales, and I remember on one of the courses I did that they were teaching us about not taking rejection personally, that only about one in 10 calls would get some kind of positive response and that we should see a rejection as being another step closer to making a sale. I see a loss in betting as another step on the way to profitability – they are a part of the process."

– Peter Webb

The long lens encourages you to look at events as if from a future perspective – some time later, looking back to now. In the moment, and in their immediate aftermath, events can appear very different to how they come across when looking back on them in a few months' time. Later, the emotional intensity lessens; insights are clarified; problems seem less overwhelming, though not less relevant; you see what went wrong, how to avoid it again, and are able to keep from overreacting. You could use a six-month lens or a three-, nine-, 12-month or even longer one if needed. It enables you to get some of the benefits and distance of hindsight almost immediately.

Keep perspective

Remember the number of bets that you make in a year and put a single loss into the context of your total number of trades. The statistics don't lie, so they can be a reassuring and trustworthy friend when you think disaster has struck and you need solid comfort. For example, if you are making 10 bets a week, that's 520 per year; a single losing bet, as a percentage of those trades, is just 0.2%.

Review: changing perspective

- Think of a loss/setback/error you have encountered – look at it with a wide lens: 'What can I learn from this?' What do you notice?

- Think of a loss/setback/error you have encountered – look at it with a long lens: go six months into the future and imagine looking back on the event. What do you notice?

Be optimistic

Cognitive psychologists suggest that an individual's 'explanatory style' (how they explain events to themselves) can be a significant factor in influencing their level of performance.

The research done by Martin Seligman (*Learned Optimism*, 1990) suggests that individuals with an optimistic explanatory style not only consistently outperform those with a pessimistic explanatory style but are also happier and live longer. Seligman's work is essentially based on 'attribution theory', which is the study of how people explain good and bad events that happen in their lives. An individual's explanatory style can be used to determine their level of optimism or pessimism.

Seligman's work covered three core 'dimensions' in people's interpretation of both negative and positive events which, it has been suggested, ultimately determine optimism or pessimism in explanatory style:

- personalisation (Ps) – how personally people take events

- permanence (Pm) – the time in which the person 'dwells' on the event; e.g. after a loss, how long you keep thinking about it for before you let go of it and move on

- pervasiveness (Pv) – how much the event impacts outside of the initial situation, e.g. if you have a tough time in betting on an event and incur a big loss do you manage to keep your frustrations within your betting or do you carry them with you into family life?

An optimistic explanatory style, particularly about bad events, encourages perseverance: pessimistic people are more likely to lose confidence and motivation after a poor performance than optimists. With pessimistic people, when a negative event occurs – for example, a big loss or losing streak; making an error; and so on – then their explanatory style promotes less perseverance, and maybe results in these people not achieving their full potential.

It pays to be optimistic

"It's significant to note that one can't *not* make explanations about the events that happen in one's life; one has to do that in order to make meaning out of the world. However, the consequences of the type of explanations one makes is very different. If we tend to make more optimistic explanations about events, then we'll be more successful in the long run than if we tend to make more pessimistic explanations."

– Jeffery Hodges, *Sportsmind*

Dust yourself off and go again

"When things do go against you, you just have to dust yourself off, not dwell on it and start the next day with a clean sheet, without chasing the day before."

– WW, sports trader

Taking action

Now you have read this section, take time to write a few notes, the key points, then consider how they apply to you in your own sports betting, before finally thinking about how you can take action.

Notes

How does this apply to me?

How can I take action?

7 Control the Frequency and Size of Your Bets

Q. *"Why do you feel so few people are able to achieve long term success and profitability in sports betting?*

A. *" 'They bet too much and too often.' "*

– Bill Esdaile, interview

In this chapter:

- Controlling the frequency of your betting
- Controlling the size of your betting

Controlling the frequency of your betting

"Do not confuse activity with achievement."

– John Wooden, legendary NCAA basketball coach

Over betting is a common problem in sports betting and can be seen in the huge turnover that many punters have. Over betting is not a desirable behaviour if you are to return consistent profits. If you're having problems and analyse your betting results carefully, you will often find that a significant number of losses are incurred through over betting. These bets are rarely well selected and researched. They tend to arise from over-enthusiasm, overconfidence, frustration, anger and – most often of all – boredom.

To reduce a harmful betting frequency, you first need to ask yourself why you're over betting. Then you need to have a solution, an alternative response in place, to match up with it, and to help you reduce or cease betting.

Let's look at some of the most common reasons why people bet too frequently, and some suggestions as to how you can change and improve your betting should any of them apply to you.

> **You can always find a reason to place a bet – but is it a good one?**
>
> **"A typical flaw in someone's psychological approach is a tendency to bet too often. Because they are doing lots of research they usually have opinions on the likely outcome of most events. But betting too often is almost inevitably going to result in losses. You need to develop the discipline to only bet when all or most of the key success factors in your system apply. This will mean you will have periods without making a bet. If you are unable to cope with this psychologically, and find you need to bet regularly, then perhaps consider developing a differential staking system. This would see you bet a very small percentage of your system stake on bets that do not meet all of your strategic criteria."**
>
> **– Keith Sobey**

Gambling and excitement

Reason: You are betting for excitement and for fun rather than for profit, much the same as most people who play in the casino.

Solution: If your goal is purely to have fun and to create excitement, then you need to accept the fact that long-term profitability is unlikely. If you want profitability from your betting, then you need to make a shift in your motives and goals away from fun and excitement towards a more professional and structured approach with trading profitability as your desired outcome.

No defined strategy

Reason: You have no defined betting strategy. Therefore there are no parameters to determine when you should bet or not. Any given sporting event and any market seems to provide an opportunity to have a bet. This opens the door to emotionally driven betting, not to mention all the other problems of, in effect, entering a battlefield without armour, weapon or plan.

Solution: The most important area that you can focus on is to develop a betting strategy with a positive expectancy. This will help you to define where your betting opportunities are and assist you in becoming more selective with your betting. (*See: 'Creating your betting strategy', page 41.*)

Bet when you have a reason to bet

"Bet when you have a reason to bet, not just because a betting opportunity is about to begin. Your best bets will be struck when you come across a proposition that appeals to you. Your worst bets will be struck because you are rushing to get on before it is too late."

– Bruce Millington, in *The Definitive Guide to Betting on Sports*

Boredom

Reason: This is a big factor and is often evident where people have a lot of time in which to place bets, or where there is little real activity in the sports the person is betting on (and so they go elsewhere to bet instead). However, these situations present you with the challenge of being patient and staying out of the market. For some people this is very difficult.

Solution: You need to balance your keenness for wanting to bet on anything that moves with the need to develop your discipline. Patience is a great skill. Do not see a lack of betting as time wasted, but rather as time well spent in developing the skill of patience. Anyone can place a bet; keeping out of the market and not betting is far more difficult. Being able to do this is vitally important. If you can't, you aren't really in control, but are at the mercy of those rival bettors who can exercise such patience.

Pro wisdom

"Don't bet just for the sake of having a bet. If you have to look hard for an opportunity, then it just isn't there."

– Matt Finnigan

"You should never feel obliged to do anything. Doing nothing can be better than doing something."

– Peter Webb

You need to make money

Reason: You are in a desperate financial situation and you need to make money. This is one of the worst situations to be in, and brings with it some of the least helpful emotions for betting. It is almost impossible to gamble with anything approaching professionalism in such a situation.

Solution: You must stop betting till the situation is solved by some other means.

Over enthusiasm

Reason: Enthusiasm is infectious and affects everyone at some point. People who are entering new sports or markets, or who are using new methodologies or software, are particularly prone to over enthusiasm. Whilst this enthusiasm is undoubtedly positive, there is also the dark side to consider: engagement can quickly become enslavement, and mere hunting for any opportunity to put a bet on.

Solution: Maintain your enthusiasm but redirect it towards developing your ability to *bet your strategy* when good opportunities appear and to developing the discipline required to do just this. If you have to bet, consider doing so with very small stakes. Also, consider using your enthusiasm to do any reading or development work that may be required or any other betting-specific tasks.

World Cup fever

"During the World Cup, a friend and I each put some money into a joint Betfair account to trade for the entire tournament. We put £100 in between us, with the objective of doubling our money during the tournament (approximately £3 per day). After the first week we were on £140. But instead of building this up steadily again, our £40 profit was wiped out chasing two games on the same day: Australia v Ghana, and Cameroon v Denmark. If we had stayed with our strategy of not risking more than 10% of our original stake, we would have continued to be successful. At the end of the World Cup, we ended up only making around £3."

– Barrie Compton, sports trader

Lack of patience

Reason: I liken the nature of the work of sports betting to that of police officers or special forces soldiers (without the physical risks) in a stake-out or observation post. It consists of prolonged periods of patience, waiting for a few brief moments of execution.

Understanding that having a bet on is only one part of the betting cycle is key. Preparation and monitoring come before placing a bet, and evaluation comes afterwards.

Solution: Some people are by nature more patient than others. However, this may not always transfer into trading. It can bring out the Mr Hyde in us. As patience is at the root of a number of these problems, let's round out this section by looking at it in more depth in the following exercise.

Put it into practice: developing the skill of patience

In the *Sports Betting to Win* survey, the issue of patience was quite prevalent. Patience is a key quality required for success in sports betting. Here are some key ways in which you can develop greater patience.

1. Develop positive beliefs about being patient.

Your beliefs and expectations about betting opportunities will have a behavioural effect on your patience levels.

Beliefs of impatient people may include:

- I have to have a bet on
- I have to bet on every race/game/event to be successful
- Not betting is a wasted opportunity
- A bet is better than no bet.

Beliefs required for patient betting may include:

- You don't have to bet on everything to make money
- You don't have to have a bet on to be betting – research and monitoring are a part of the betting process too
- The betting markets will give you limitless opportunities over time – you don't know when they will come, but they will come
- Not betting can be great betting
- Flawless execution requires the execution of strategy bets only
- All good things come to those who wait.

2. Recognise that actually placing a bet is only a part of the betting process and that it is likely that you will spend a large amount of your time in the research and planning stage, and in watching/waiting and evaluating stages.

3. Expectations – you need to develop realistic expectations about what you want from your betting and how quickly these outcomes will most likely take.

4. Spend a betting session just watching the market, resisting the urge to bet; or give yourself a target of reducing your number of bets you make in a given period to half to make you more selective and patient. This can be a very powerful strategy in helping to instil your belief that you can be patient and that you don't have to have a bet.

> ### The best bet can be not to bet
>
> **"I can do my reading and research, read Kevin Pullein's column and if at the end of it all the conclusion is that it is a no bet – that is a bet."**
>
> – Wally Pyrah

In revenge

Reason: where people have lost money there is often an urge to 'get my money back'. Whilst the intention of such a thought is positive, the ensuing behaviour is often not: generally it entails reckless, unplanned betting.

Solution: Where you have had a big loss or lost a large amount of money through a series of bets you may wish to incorporate a ritual to take a time out. This time out allows you time to readdress your mental state and to refocus etc. but also, and most importantly, breaks the behavioural pattern of *lose money – feel angry – get money back*. The time out causes a break in the pattern and enables you to refocus.

The costs of over betting

There are real costs to over betting in terms of:

- the extra money you are losing, commission charges, spreads being paid

- the emotional frustration of knowing that you are over betting

- the longer-term damage incurred through taking bets that are not a part of your betting strategy, and therefore ingraining and practising ill-discipline.

These costs have short- and longer-term impact on your betting performance and profitability. Over betting should be carefully monitored. Be aware of the particular circumstances when you are more prone to over betting and monitor these situations carefully as they arise. Take action according to what is driving your behaviour.

Put it into practice: reducing over betting

1. Reflect on your betting – use your logs/journals – and identify the key times/situations when you are prone to over betting.

2. Review the common causes of over betting and their solutions in this chapter and apply any that are appropriate as preventative measures.

3. Make a note of where your 'risk' of over betting is highest and most likely to occur. For each of these situations decide how you will monitor if you start to over bet and what you will do once you have recognised it. It may be as simple as stopping and taking some time out to slow down and reflect on what has happened.

Control the size of your bets: size matters

Alongside betting too frequently, taking too much risk – staking too big – is another of the betting behaviours that underpins many people's lack of success and profitability. It probably accounts for the majority of punters who suffer big losses and wipe out their betting banks quickly.

The actual size of the stake itself is not the key concern. Rather, it is this amount in relation to the betting bank, and in turn, the betting bank to the size of a bettor's personal wealth.

The discipline of managing your risk and staking appropriately is absolutely fundamental to success in sports betting. Ultimately you can only bet if you have a betting bank, so preservation of capital is key. Managing risk also helps you to manage emotion. Significant risk can lead to big wins and overconfidence and adrenaline-based betting, whilst big losses create anger and frustration and revenge betting.

Why do people bet too big? What can they do about it?

Lack of knowledge

"Most people who start out in sports betting take way too much risk."

– Peter Webb

Many people enter the world of sports betting with little or limited experience, training or knowledge, particularly of risk management and staking. People tend to focus on trying to find a winning strategy first and pay less attention to staking. Some people blindly follow the latest winning tipster, and want to make big money quickly by placing large bets based on their current form.

There are many different approaches and strategies to staking. You have to find one that sits well with you and your style of betting. Perhaps the most important factor, and irrelevant of the specifics of the strategy employed, is that any staking plan should be focused on ensuring that you stay in the game, that your capital is preserved over time, and that you are not wiped out after a few losses.

Solution: Take time to learn about different staking systems. Find one that appeals to you and that has good capital-preservation parameters. Try it out and make any appropriate changes over time based on the feedback you get from your betting results. Commit to sticking to your staking plan.

Recovering losses

When people have lost money, as we saw earlier, they are willing to incur bigger risk in order to recover that loss. They become risk seeking, and are more susceptible to being guided by their emotions.

Solution: The time following a big loss or a string of losses is a potentially dangerous one, with a window of opportunity for revenge betting to occur. Be conscious of these times and develop an awareness of how you feel during them. If your feelings are those of anger and your primary motivation is to get your money back as quickly as is possible then you are undoubtedly in the wrong state of mind to place a rational bet. So you should not bet. Take a break, and do not return to betting until you are in a more focused, and calmer, state. This might take minutes, hours or days, depending on the magnitude of the event.

Overconfidence

Overconfidence is the peculiar root of much in the way of over staking. After all, if a sure thing is a sure thing, why not painlessly double one's winnings with a doubled-up stake (even if it cheerfully disregards all risk controls)? This is a much more prevalent and tempting proposal than mere over betting out of overconfidence (discussed earlier in this chapter), as it can assault the bettor at any point.

In sports betting, it's actually probably safer to be lacking in confidence than it is to be over confident. If you're anxious, you're unlikely to be making much money, but you certainly won't be losing too much. Betting when you are in a state of overconfidence can have a significant impact on your betting bank – at best you will get big positive up swings, at worst, and most likely over time, you will get massive losses.

Can you think of times when you have experienced overconfidence in your betting?

What was the result?

Overconfidence or at least high confidence is needed for us to take on challenges and so is useful in one form. However, we need to be mindful of the fine distinction between high confidence and overconfidence.

Solution: The first step is to identify when you are at risk of overconfidence and to then put in place specific actions to implement in those particular circumstances.

Reflect on your own betting. When are you most prone to overconfidence?

In my experience there are two key events that particularly give rise to strong levels of overconfidence:

- a win that is significantly greater than normal

- when you are on a winning run.

Understanding that these two particular situations can lead to overconfidence means that we should classify them as high risk. If a part of being successful at sports betting is about managing risk then betting is definitely about managing overconfidence. Now if those two situations trigger overconfidence, then building some protocol around them may be very useful. The first element is awareness – knowing the situations and the signs.

When you are getting overconfident, how do you know?

Signs that you are getting overconfident may include:

- wanting to place bigger bets

- betting more frequently than usual

- placing bets that are non-strategy bets and have little verifiable edge in the market

- not doing your preparation and/or evaluation

- generally putting less time and effort into your betting

- thoughts of glory, delusions of being a new betting master; that this is easy, that you have cracked it, that you cannot lose or be beaten – all thoughts, however packaged, are warning signs.

If you notice yourself getting overconfident then what action can you take?

Overconfidence is a strong and powerful emotion. It is intense. It is fuelled by events and by itself. It therefore carries momentum. One of the fundamental strategies that you should consider employing, therefore, is to break its momentum by stopping betting.

Take time out and evaluate your betting, your behaviours and actions. Then re-read/assess your betting strategy and look at how you will implement it going forward. If you really feel that you cannot stick to your strategy then not trading until these feelings subside may be the best trade of all.

Betting for excitement is another common cause of betting with improper stakes. See the advice in the first half of the chapter relating to over betting caused by the same issues.

Taking action

Now you have read this section take time to write a few notes, the key points, then consider how they apply to you in your own sports betting, before finally thinking about how you can take action.

Notes
....

How does this apply to me?
....

How can I take action?
....

8 Manage Your Emotions

"Emotions will play a big part in our success and it's how we condition them that will determine whether we will be successful, both in sports betting, and in life."

– Matt Finnigan

In this chapter:

- How emotions affect your betting results
- Understanding how emotions are created
- Developing emotional awareness
- Creating performance-enhancing emotions
- Dealing with performance-limiting emotions

How emotions affect your betting results

Why is it that top-class sportspeople miss a short putt to win a tournament or miss vital penalties in football games when they can make those shots with exceptionally high success rates in practice? What changes?

How they are feeling – their emotional state.

How you feel affects how you perform. Can you think of a time in your life – maybe in sports, an exam, an interview, a performance of some sort – where you felt good, positive, focused and performed well; and likewise where maybe nerves, anxiety, fatigue, or self-doubt stopped you from performing to your potential?

Emotions underpin performance and results

When you learn how to manage your emotions you learn how to manage your behaviour, control your performance and improve your results.

Understanding how emotions are created

Emotions are affects; they are the psychological and physiological consequences of things you have done or are doing, and they are the connecting force between the mind and the body.

Each emotional state has a 'blueprint' to it – a set of mental and physiological conditions that are apparent. For example, for the states of confidence and anxiety the blueprints may look something like the ones below:

Emotional blueprints for confidence and anxiety

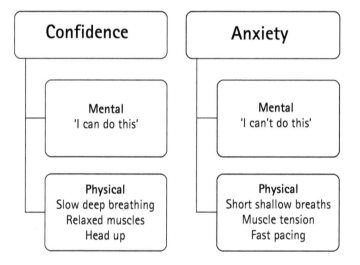

 Review: emotional blueprints

Think of some of the key emotions that you feel whilst you are betting. Write them down.

Now for each of them identify the mental and physical components – the blueprint – for each.

Emotions are dynamic processes – how you feel changes regularly throughout the day, experiencing different moods as you respond to events around you and your physical feelings of hunger and tiredness, etc. What is the purpose of emotions? Emotions serve to get us 'in motion', to mobilise us, to enable the body to respond. Below is a sample of emotions and how they enable you to act:

Emotion	Action enabled
Anger	Attack, force, strike out
Fear	Retreat, withdraw
Challenge	Engage, pursue
Love	Nourish, care for, protect

Your performance in betting, in your relationships, in sport and in all arenas, is profoundly influenced by your feelings. How you feel affects how you perform and the results that you get. Performance is state dependent.

It is important to recognise, though, that these feelings don't just happen to you. They are choices and conditioned responses. Looking at emotions from a cognitive perspective, they are the result of your mindset. They arise out of how you tend to think, your beliefs and your most common perceptions. Once an emotional response has been activated in response to an event enough times it becomes conditioned and automatic. This is why sometimes it can appear that our emotions just happen to us without much in the way of interpretation or process – a shortcut from the event to the emotion has been created. This is known as stimulus-response conditioning.

❝Performance is state dependent.❞

Cognitive model showing how mindset drives emotion

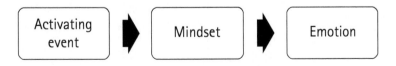

Stimulus–response conditioning: Pavlov's dogs

Ivan Pavlov was a noted Russian physiologist who went on to win the 1904 Nobel Prize for his work studying digestive processes. In a now famous series of experiments, Pavlov exposed dogs to the sound of a ticking metronome immediately before presenting them with food. After several trials, Pavlov noted that the dogs would begin to salivate on hearing the metronome alone – they associated the sound of the metronome with being presented with food, and this prompted the automatic activation of the dogs' salivary secretion. The reaction (salivating) had become conditioned to the stimulus (the metronome) – in the absence of food.

Developing emotional awareness

Emotions are natural and are a part of being human. It is important to recognise that learning to identify and understand your emotions is more important, in most cases, than trying to suppress or control them. One of the most important areas to develop awareness in is in assessing which of the emotions you experience are performance-enhancing, as against those which are performance-limiting, and being able to recognise which of these you are experiencing at any given time.

Review: performance-enhancing and performance-limiting states

Make a list of the states that you feel help you to perform well in your betting and those that you feel detract from your performance

Performance-enhancing betting states

....

....

....

....

Performance-limiting betting states

....

....

....

....

It is important to start to look at states as drivers of behaviour and performance.

For each of the states you have listed, connect it to a behaviour that occurs when you are in that state. For example: confidence = back my judgement. Or: frustration = take bets that I shouldn't do.

Examples of performance enhancing emotions might include:

- confident

- focused

- relaxed

- calm

- energised.

Examples of performance limiting emotions might include:

- anger

- frustration

- fear

- tiredness

- boredom.

Here are some useful questions that you can ask yourself to identify how you are feeling at any given time. They may help you attain a high level of emotional awareness.

- How are you feeling right now?

- What is the effect of how you are feeling on your behaviour?

- Why might I be feeling this way? What is the message behind the emotion?

- What am I thinking and what is happening physiologically to maintain my current state?

- How would I rather be feeling?

- What do I want to change to feel how I want to now?

A really simple and very practical but powerful strategy that I have used very successfully with many people is to get them to 'check in'.

Put it into practice: check in

Imagine that 10 is how would you like to be feeling right now and that 0 is the other end of the spectrum.

Where are you right now?

0 ⟵———————————————⟶ 10

How would you rather be feeling?

What do you need to change to have that feeling now?

Creating performance-enhancing emotions

In sport you will often hear about people being in the zone, and psychologists will often talk about being in flow. Both of these are references to emotional states that enable a person to be at their best; they are states that support peak performance. Typically these are described using words such as:

- physically and mentally relaxed

- alert

- feeling in control

- calm

- energised

- positive

- focused

- confident

- effortless

- automatic.

In *Stress for Success*, James E. Loehr explains that the zone, or Ideal Performance State as he refers to it, "is a learnt response and is a highly unique and specific response to stress with a high emotional content. It is linked to underlying physiological and neurological events and enables you to express your talents and skills to the best of your ability."

Review: identifying your ideal performance state

Use the following questions to help you to identify the 'blueprint' for how you feel when you are at your best.

- How is my physiology in that state? How is my breathing? How is my muscle tension? How is my heart rate?
- How is my body language? Gestures? Facial expression?
- How are my energy levels? Tired? Hungry? Dehydrated?
- What thoughts do I have?
- What images do I have/create?

By managing your physiology and your thoughts you can begin to access this ideal state on demand.

Creating confidence

Of all the performance-enhancing emotions, confidence is the one that is most talked about and is most sought after. Confidence is without doubt a big factor in how people perform. An unshakeable confidence and self-belief is critical to betting success, and is important in not just being able to execute your strategy effectively and being able to perform to your potential, but also in how you respond to and recover from losses, setbacks, and errors.

Review: Confidence self-assessment

How confident are you in your betting?

On a 0-10 scale, with 0 being no confidence and 10 being very confident, where would you put yourself?

0  10

What would it take to score higher?

Confidence in betting is twofold. Firstly, there is confidence in your betting plan/strategy (outer game), and secondly in your ability to execute your plan, to be disciplined (inner game). The two are obviously inextricably linked, and working on both is the key to achieving a core of confidence that allows your bets to be executed effectively.

Confidence can mean different things to different people. For most, being confident would include feeling that you are likely to make money, that you are executing your strategy without hesitation, and that you believe that on any given bet you are more likely to make money than lose it. In most cases, it would probably be linked (for better or worse, as we have discussed) to how much money you are making.

Confidence is key

"Above all, you must have faith in the system of betting you have developed."

– Keith Sobey

"You have to back your judgement to be right or wrong."

– Wally Pyrah

I would encourage you to see confidence not as something mystical or entirely dependent on how much money you are making but as a skill to be developed and a process to be implemented. Confidence is an emotional state, and therefore it has a 'blueprint'. Hence, by developing your ability to manage your thoughts, mental images and your physiology, body language, energy levels and even the way you look and dress, you can learn to manage your levels of confidence.

Confidence is a choice.

Put it into practice: building a core of confidence

Below are five keys to developing and sustaining greater confidence in your sports betting.

1. Develop competence

Confidence is based significantly upon competence, i.e. having the skills, abilities, knowledge and understanding to achieve the task being attempted. Developing competence is the number one way of developing confidence.

2. Concentrate on the process and what is controllable, not the outcome

It is the linking of confidence to money that causes such emotional ups and downs for people. It is important to recognise that how much money you make or lose is the outcome of how well you bet, whilst being confident is a process that leads to an outcome. It is possible to bet badly, take excessive risk, punt, and make good money – should that give you great confidence? Confidence should ideally be linked to good betting behaviours and performance, which are far more under your control; and being in control adds to the feeling of confidence.

"Confidence is that space where you feel free to focus on only those things that you can control."

– Jerry Lynch, *The Way of the Champion*

3. Prepare

Going into any event, whether it be betting, a sports event, a job interview or giving a public speech, being fully prepared can help significantly to provide additional feelings of confidence. Taking time to prepare and research, looking at 'what if?' scenarios and any possible eventualities and how you might react will all help.

4. Develop discipline

Trusting in yourself to be able to follow your betting strategy/rules, and manage your money/risk, is a core underlying component of confidence. When you doubt your discipline and ability to act in ways that are positive, it causes anxiety and hesitation.

5. Believe in your strategy

Where you deeply believe in your strategy and its ability to make profits over time, you will feel substantially more confident. Developing a strategy that has a positive expectancy and continually evaluating its performance and refining it as appropriate are absolutely essential.

"Over the course of a year I will bet on about 9,000-10,000 horse races and at the end of each day's racing I will generally be up; at the end of a week I will most probably be up; at the end of each month and the end of the year I will be up."

– Peter Webb

Dealing with performance-limiting emotions positively

There will be times in your betting when you will experience emotions that are not conducive to making good betting decisions and performing to your best. Trying to do something when you are not in the right state is like putting your foot on the accelerator when the car is not in gear – lots of revs, but you don't go anywhere.

Limiting emotions have an adverse effect on your performance because they do not enable you to effectively make the decisions and perform the actions that are required for betting in a disciplined way. When you experience emotions such as anger, fear, frustration and any of those that create stress, you get changes in your body chemistry that affect your ability to perform. Under these conditions, the blood flow to the cortex within the brain (the rational part of the brain required for logical thinking and objective decision-making) is restricted. This results in cortical inhibition, a process of shutting down of the 'smart brain', leaving you with access only to your emotional centres. The result of this is that you are now betting driven by your emotions and not your strategy.

When you are in such states your ability to perform logical betting processes is dramatically compromised and the risk of poor quality, undisciplined betting is increased.

The behavioural effects of being in some of the key limiting emotional states include:

Emotional state	Behaviour
Frustration, impatience and overconfidence	Over betting, wanting to be involved, trying to make things happen
Fear, anxiety	Not betting when there are good opportunities, protecting wins/losses
Anger	Losing it, revenge betting, chasing losses, trying to get even
Overconfidence	Over betting and taking more risk

 Put it into practice: dealing with negative states positively

1. Emotions as messengers

Think of emotions as messengers.

Ask 'What is the message behind this emotion?'

In doing so you are moving away from purely focusing on *what* you are feeling to *why* you are feeling. Once you have identified the emotion and the reason why you are feeling it then you are ready to take action on the feedback you have received.

2. Go into neutral

When you are in a negatively charged state it can be extremely difficult to switch from that state straight into a positive one. To help you to transition from a negative state into a more positive state it can be very useful to go into a 'neutral' state first. Try this very simple exercise to achieve a 'neutral state' and then when you have achieved this and feel ready, you can manage your mental and physical processes to shift into a performance-enhancing emotional state.

First – focus on your heart. You may find it easier to do this by placing a hand on your heart, or by looking towards your heart area, or even by listening to your heartbeat.

Secondly – breathe in to a count of five and out to a count of five. This rhythm has been proven by cardiac research at the Heartmath Institute in the USA to be very powerful in achieving positive physiological status. It may feel uncomfortable at first, so perseverance and practice are key.

Keep focused on the heart and perform the breathing for as long as you need to until you can feel that you are calmer and ready to shift to a more positive state.

3. Take time out

Think of a time when you experienced a limiting emotional state. Did it last for ever? No. At some point your emotional state will shift and over time you will return to more positive states. Sometimes taking a 'time out' whether a short or a longer one, can be the most effective way of reducing losses in the short term and getting your head together to return to betting with a more positive and focused mindset.

4. Bet when you are at your best

If you are experiencing an emotional state that you know will have an adverse effect on your betting decision making and discipline then the simplest and most important advice is to not bet. The risk of losing money is too high. Choose when to bet carefully; not when you are upset, tired, have something on your mind, or can't focus 100% on what you are doing. There will be plenty of other opportunities in the future.

Staying calm when the pressure is on

There are times in betting when the heat is really on and the sensation of pressure is high – for example, when you are betting in-running in a fast moving market.

These situations can often be referred to as critical moments – moments where how you think, feel, behave and therefore perform will have significant consequences on the outcome. In sport, great athletes relish these critical moments: the clutch moments that can define a game, that can lead to victory or loss. The kicker in rugby who steps up to take the final penalty kick or drop goal to win the game; the footballers who step-up to take the penalties in the cup final; the golfer who has to make the final putt to win the tournament; the tennis player serving to win a grand slam.

In betting, it is the person who suddenly has to deal with a large betting position in a market that has just become more volatile; the person who has to cut his position as the market moves quickly against them; the person who reacts quickly and decisively to enter the market as a good betting opportunity appears; the person who sticks to his strategy through ups and downs seeing the bet out to its conclusion; or the person who makes a mistake that leaves them in an undesirable situation, who then calmly deals with it and gets the best achievable outcome.

When the pressure is on there are generally three responses that you can experience:

1. You dive – you crack under the pressure, called 'choking' in sport, and you underperform.

2. You survive – you get through.

3. You thrive – you relish the challenge of the opportunity and the pressure raises your performance.

Review: are you a critical moment performer?

Think of some high-pressure situations that you have encountered in your betting.

How did you react to them? How did you perform?

Did you dive, survive or thrive?

How you behave under pressure is a function of your competence, experience, mindset and performance skills.

Put it into practice: developing your critical moment performance

Identify as many specific critical moments as you can that may occur in your betting and plan out what you will do if they should occur. It can be very useful to mentally run through, to mentally rehearse, these situations, creating a video in your mind of how you will perform in them.

Where possible, develop the skills and abilities that will help you to perform well in these situations. Competence is, as we saw earlier, key to confidence. Knowing that you have what it takes to deal with these moments will be significant in how well you perform.

Focus only on those aspects of performance that are under your control.

Slow down. Slow down your breathing, speed of movement, how quickly you are talking and thinking. Under pressure the natural tendency is to speed up.

Learn from every critical moment that you encounter, build your knowledge bank and your level of experience and utilise these to improve your performance in the future.

Fear

The old enemy of confidence is fear, and fear can be a very limiting emotion when it comes to betting. What are we most afraid of apart from dying and public speaking? In betting the these fears are:

- fear of the unknown

- fear of losing money

- fear of missing out on an opportunity

- fear of being wrong

- fear of leaving money on the table.

(Adapted from *Trading in the Zone*, by Mark Douglas.)

Fear can be thought of as F.E.A.R. – False Evidence Appearing Real – as it is purely a subjective feeling. Fear only exists in the past and in the future as we mentally generate thoughts and play images that create it – replaying the bet we just lost on, or pre-playing a scenario of losing money on the upcoming one. One of the keys to overcoming feelings of fear is to 'be in the moment': to focus on what is happening here and now and to act accordingly – to execute your plan, to make the right decisions right now.

Put it into practice: embracing fear

Fear of the unknown

Embrace and get comfortable with uncertainty. Accept that you don't need to know what is going to happen to make money.

Fear of losing money

Accepting that losses are a part of betting is the first part of overcoming this fear and then secondly managing your risk appropriately, such that at any given time you are emotionally and financially comfortable with taking that loss.

Fear of missing out on an opportunity

The betting markets offer endless opportunities over time and you do not need to bet on every single one to achieve your goals. Adopting this belief is key to managing this fear.

Fear of being wrong

This is a fear driven by your ego. Ask yourself, 'What is more important – being right or making money?' Betting is a game of probabilities, a game with high levels of uncertainty, and so being 'right' is not going to happen 100% of the time. Let go of the need to get the outcome right and focus on getting the process right.

Fear of leaving money on the table

For people who trade spreads or bet in-play the fear of leaving money on the table is what can stop you from getting out of a bet at a price because you don't want to get out and then see the price go further in your direction and losing out on the money you could have made. It is important to see sports trading as an 'in and out' strategic process based on probability, planning and preparation, and with the intention of capturing moments within the market – much like a photographer at a sports event – and not becoming obsessed with trying to capture whole moves which is highly unlikely and very risky.

Taking action

Now you have read this section take time to write a few notes, the key points, then consider how they apply to you in your own sports betting, before finally thinking about how you can take action.

Notes

How does this apply to me?

How can I take action?

9 Manage the Ups and the Downs

"Life is a rollercoaster, just gotta ride it."

— Ronan Keating, Boyzone

In this chapter:

Losing streaks and the downside of sports betting

The winning run and when betting is great

Sports betting is a rollercoaster

If you stay in sports betting for long enough then one thing is certain – you will experience strings of wins and strings of losses; ups and downs. The most important factor is not whether you will experience these highs and lows but how you will deal with them when they arise. David Paul, a good friend of mine who is a successful financial trader, explains this as being able to deal with the 'clusters'. Clusters are where events group themselves together, the string of heads or tails in a coin toss, the run of reds on a roulette wheel, the run of perceived good luck or bad luck we are having, our strings of betting wins and losses. He suggests that trading is not so much a test of your analytical ability but more a test of your character. These two extremes of experience are critical times. Both can create the opportunity either for growth, development and improved performance – or for ill-discipline, with disastrous results.

> *"The difference between a professional and an amateur is not necessarily the ability to analyse a match, it's how they handle the emotions of a sustained losing period."*
>
> – Matt Finnigan

Losing streaks and the downside of sports betting

Failure and adversity enable success

> *"That which does not kill us makes us stronger."*
>
> – Friedrich Nietzsche

Anyone who bets for long enough, no matter how experienced and skilled they are, is likely to go through tough periods at some point. These periods can be extended, either in time or in the amount of money lost. Some people bounce back from these periods; others don't.

Periods of difficulty or loss in betting have potentially dangerous consequences as an outcome of the coping strategies that people employ, and as such it is important that you develop strategies to deal with them that maintain your discipline, focus and confidence.

The possible effects of a period of loss include:

- losing confidence in your strategy

- making radical changes to your approach

- becoming obsessed with losses

- increasing your bet size and taking more risk in order to get out of the situation quickly

- becoming despondent and low in mental energy.

The phrase 'mental toughness' is used a lot in sports and in life in general. In most cases we are looking largely at someone's resilience. Resilience is the capacity to survive or thrive in adversity, enduring and overcoming the experience of unfortunate or stressful events. In betting, that tends to be losses, setbacks and errors.

Betting presents you with many challenges, pressure and often adversity. People lose, they make mistakes, they encounter tough periods, they go through drawdown and they have setbacks. What separates those who bounce back, who keep going and eventually make it through and back to profitability, from those who get beaten by their situation? Toughness – resilience is the deciding factor.

The big challenge

"To overcome long losing runs and still manage your bankroll is the biggest challenge in sports betting."

– Diego Cassanova

"The main challenges in sports betting are certainly the staying power and discipline needed to stick to your plan when things are going against you and you hit that inevitable losing run."

– Pete Nordsted

I remember once reading about New Zealand triathlete Hamish Carter, who was determined to win his Olympics event in Sydney in 2000. He was a very talented athlete and trained really hard and dedicated his whole life to the achievement of that goal. Imagine, then, his disappointment at finishing 26th.

Following that setback, he decided to re-evaluate his whole training process, lifestyle, psychology – everything. He then set about on another four-year training cycle, working towards the 2004 games in Athens. At those games he finished first.

Upon achieving his goal – his dream – he categorically stated that it had taken that loss in 2000 to give him the drive to really make some changes in his approach, and that had given him the mental toughness to be able to win in 2004.

In his own words: "The key to success is failure. If I didn't have Sydney to wallow in, I wouldn't have won in Athens. It [Sydney] was the worst day of my life, but one of the most important."

Tough times make tough people. Getting through these times is often a function of desire and passion to achieve the end goal, self-belief and the mental and physical resilience to keep going and endure this period. Having worked with many successful people in the financial and sports markets I can testify that pretty much without exception all have endured periods of challenge, some quite extreme, before achieving their success, and that all with the benefit of hindsight can look on those events now as key and even defining moments in their journey to achieving their goals.

Psychological resilience is key to success

"I can think of no psychological characteristic more important to long-term success than psychological resilience. Resilience has been defined in a number of ways, sometimes as a process, other times as a trait. In all cases, resilience presumes exposure to stressful conditions and an ability to maintain high levels of social, emotional, and vocational functioning throughout this exposure."

– Brett Steenbarger, psychiatrist, trading coach

When things don't seem to work – be proactive!

Sometimes when you are betting it can feel that nothing is working, that everything and everyone is against you and that you are destined to lose money. I am sure that many of you have experienced that feeling. And it is perfectly natural . . . but what do you do when you are in that situation?

It is easy to get into a downward spiral, getting more and more negative, which in turn makes successful betting even more difficult. And then the results still don't come, and so it continues off into the land of doom and gloom.

This prevails until something happens, and you make some money market, an act of randomness occurs, you profit and your mood is lifted and promotes your rise back upwards.

The question is, though, how long do you wait for that random event to provide some profit and the psychological pick up? In this situation you are like a sailing boat on the ocean with no rudder, at the mercy of the wind and waves; in fact you are in a psychological state of helplessness which has been much studied by the prominent American psychologist Martin Seligman.

Advice from the pros

"From a practical perspective, dealing with losses is very difficult to overcome. When on a winning run, sports betting is easy and fun; when things go badly it can quickly become depressing and stressful and that changes the outlook. You can quickly find yourself chasing to get back to where you were. It is really important not to abandon your processes – don't change what you are doing drastically – it could be just a random streak."

– Tony Hargraves

"Losing punters find it hard to stomach losing runs and quickly lose confidence in the strategy or tactics they are using. This is where emotions take over and we feel vulnerable. How you channel these emotions will determine how successful you are going to be long-term."

– Matt Finnigan

Have you ever had a car that broke down? If so, what was your attitude and approach? Did you view it as though the whole car was broken, and did you wait for some random event to occur and for the car to start working again? Probably not... You may have tried to identify where the problem was specifically, knowing that it was hardly likely to be the whole car that was broken but rather a part of the car. And this may have been done by yourself or with the help of a professional in the automotive industry. Problem identified, you then decided to get it fixed and soon got back driving.

The key thing is that you were *active* in getting the problem resolved, that you looked to identify where the *specific* challenge was and then were able to resolve the issue and move forward.

When you are having a tough time in your betting it is not the whole world or the whole of you that is suddenly not working. You need to take a proactive approach to resolving the challenge that you are facing and aim to identify the specific areas in which your performance is being affected.

> *"If you want to see a great fighter at his best then watch him when he is getting beat."*
>
> – Sugar Ray Robinson

Consider what your reaction has been when faced with such situations in your betting. Do you suffer from helplessness and wait for random events to bail you out, or are you proactive and focused on solving the problem? People who take a more dynamic, problem-focused approach to their betting challenges are more likely to return to higher levels of performance more quickly, and will most likely have greater levels of resilience and feel more in control of their betting outcomes.

Psychological resilience is a mindset – it is about how you mentally deal with tough situations; what you choose to think and say to yourself in those events and what beliefs, attitudes and perceptions you have that underpin them. An event can be the same for many different people and yet the outcomes could all be vastly different based on their mindset. It is therefore not the events that happen to us that actually determine our results but rather our mindset and how we choose to respond.

Put it into practice: dealing with tough times and losing streaks

Evaluate – look back over your betting records and see if you can find any fundamental reasons for your change in results. The two core components that make up your betting outcomes are how you are betting and the markets you are betting on. So where there has been a drop off in results away from the norm I would assess how you have been betting (your processes), and what's been happening in the sports/markets you have bet on. Alongside this, consider whether there have been events outside of your betting that may have had an impact, e.g. moving house, work stress, financial pressure, births, marriages, deaths.

"If you lose confidence in your strategy, then re-evaluate rather than giving up on it, it might just be a blip."

– Matt Finnigan

Go back to basics – ABC betting. When nothing seems to be working and you just can't seem to get any traction in what you are doing, it is often very effective to go back to basics. Strip down what you are doing to the most simplistic of methods and approaches and focus purely on doing the basics well. As your confidence grows, you can gradually begin to return to your old ways.

Take a break. Sometimes a tough time can really drain you, and trying to work harder and harder to get out just makes you more tired and run down. Taking some time away from your betting can serve the purpose of recharging you physically but also allowing your mind to declutter and refresh and to allow you to return to your betting in better physical, mental and emotional shape, with the increased potential of betting more effectively and profitably.

The meaning of any event is the meaning that you give it. If you have a tough time and you start to say that you are in a 'slump', what does that mean to you? If being in a slump means being in a long-term negative and undesirable set of betting events, then that may not be the best label. I actively encourage people not to use that word as it often has negative connotations and can keep you trapped inside their experience as they repeatedly reinforce that you are in a slump. Be wary of your language and aim to frame the situation as positively as possible – 'I am having a bit of a challenge' or 'Things are not quite going to plan', etc.

"Of all the virtues we can learn, no trait is more essential for survival and more likely to improve the quality of life than the ability to transform adversity into an enjoyable challenge."

– Mihaly Csikszentmihaly, prominent psychologist and expert on flow and emotions

See any bad patches as temporary. A part of being resilient is having an optimistic explanatory style, as we saw in the section on handling losses, and in this case the key aspect here is keeping the permanence factor short, i.e. seeing any situation that you are in as being short term and temporary. If you expect your 'bad patch' to go on for months then guess what...it might just do.

Focus on your strengths, what you can control and what positives are occurring. List your strengths and how you can utilise them most effectively. List the aspects of your betting that are controllable by you and focus on these (planning, research, evaluation, bet selection, staking strategy etc.) and not on areas that are outside of your control. Each day list at least one – and preferably more – positives; things that have gone well, that you have enjoyed or learnt.

Monitor your mental and emotional state – check in regularly – do everything you can to maintain as high a level of state as you can. As we have seen, this has such a big impact on your performance capability. Being fed up is not an ideal state and the chances of you returning to form are minimal except being saved by market events. Be aware of your physiology and body language and monitor the quality of your self-talk, as this is a good indicator of mood.

Monitor your physical state. It is particularly important during such times to pay attention to your health and wellbeing, to make sure that you are getting good quality sleep, that you are eating well and drinking plenty of water, exercising (the best way to burn off stress) and getting some downtime to recover. When times are tough, energy expenditure is high and so you need to focus on making deposits into your energy bank with good habits.

Keep a positive perspective and expectancy. Start each day and betting session by recalling times in the past when you have performed well and achieved positive results. It is essential to keep the 'success circuits' in the brain activated in order to be able to replicate this level of performance in the future. If you are not getting the results that you want in your betting in reality and you spend significant amounts of time replaying this in your mind then you are simply programming yourself for more of the same. Focus on what you want.

Financial resilience is key to survival

"It is important to ensure that you are correctly financed to be able to carry out your plan"

– Pete Nordsted

Finances are rarely linked to resilience. However, in my opinion they are an absolutely fundamental part of it. If resilience is about being able to weather tough patches, then having a sufficiently sized betting bank is absolutely critical. In fact, for me, financial resilience may be the most important factor in betting resilience.

Financial resilience has three levels to it:

1. **Personal capital/wealth** – your personal level of financial wealth. This is important because if in betting you encounter difficult periods and challenges then your betting may not be able to 'pay you' what you would like or need. If you have sufficient personal capital then during such periods you will be able survive without the need to go into desperation mode to make money to pay bills, etc. This can have a significant impact on your success or failure. Additionally your betting bank will be allocated from your personal wealth. If your betting bank is a large proportion of your personal wealth then every loss impacts at two levels – your betting bank and your personal wealth – and that increases the pain and the emotional impact of a loss.

2. **Betting bank** – the allocation of capital you have to bet with. The size of your betting bank is most significant because it is a determinant of the size of stake that you can bet with. If your betting bank is small then either you accept this, take small risks and receive small rewards; or if you are trying to make big returns on that bank then you are essentially forced into taking large risks. Obviously taking large and excessive risks is not desirable but for most people neither is making small returns – greed and expectations that are greater than your betting bank allows for will in most cases end up in a betting style that is high risk, with high volatility of wins and losses and ultimately a highly emotional and, in most cases, negative and unprofitable experience. Having a solid betting bank allows you take risks that are appropriate AND gives you achievable monetary results.

3. **Bet size** – the amount of risk you take in your betting is a feature of you, your betting style and the size of your betting bank. Everyone has to find their own style and methodology for staking that is appropriate for them, their betting strategy and the sports and markets they are betting on. However, it is important to note that excessive risk-taking can be detrimental to making good decisions, can elevate stress levels and be a cause of fear and anxiety.

* * *

Your bet size, betting bank and personal capital should all be linked in and related to each other. The model for this may look something like the one in chapter 6 (page 94), with personal capital being the base, betting bank a proportion of that and then bet size a smaller proportion of that.

Review: financial resilience assessment

Take a moment to assess your financial resilience.

Are you financially strong?

Could you weather a tough period in your betting and still bounce back?

How long could you survive with no betting income?

What percentage of your betting bank are you risking each bet? How many losses could you incur at this rate before wiping out?

The winning run and when times are great

We all know that, when your betting results are not where you want them to be, it is not a particularly enjoyable time. Having the resilience to get through these times is critical, as we have seen. This can be a testing period and can have an impact on your ability to sustain high performance in terms of attitudes and behaviours.

However, something really interesting that I have noticed with people in betting is that another dangerous, high-risk time is actually when things are going well; and the better they are going the greater the threat. Many people work hard and achieve good results only to fall off the wagon and give large amounts of their betting bank away – sometimes all of it. Why is this?

The trappings of success

The biggest hurdle when people are being successful with their betting is making money. It can breed overconfidence, complacency, laziness, and in some cases arrogance; and any one of those emotions can drive betting behaviours that are ill-disciplined and will ultimately lead to increased frequency or size of losses.

Learn to keep what you are making

By the third day of their honeymoon in Las Vegas the newly-weds had lost all of their £1,000 gambling allowance. During the night the groom woke up and noticed a $5 chip on the bedside table that they had saved as a souvenir. Strangely the number 17 appeared to be flashing on the chip's face, and he took this as an omen.

He quickly got dressed and went downstairs to the roulette wheel in the hotel casino. He placed $5 on 17 – he hit and won $175. He let his winnings ride on 17 and made $6,125. He kept going on 17 and eventually had $7.5 million. At this point the casino manager intervened, as he was worried that the casino would not be able to pay out if he hit 17 again.

The groom decided to go downtown to a bigger casino to continue playing. He put all of his winnings on 17 and won $262 million. Ecstatic, he let his winnings ride further on 17. But this time it landed on 18 and he lost everything. Broke and dejected, the groom walked the three miles back to his hotel.

On his return, the bride asked where he had been, to which he replied: playing roulette.

"How did you do?" she asked.

How much did he say he had lost? $

    a. $5 – the value of the chip

    b. $0 – he was no worse off

    c. $262 million – the amount he could have cashed

What was your answer?

There isn't a right or wrong one. But what this scenario does is reveal your underlying attitude to money gained. The closer you get in your thinking to answer c, the better. And if you haven't got as far as thinking like answer a, you need to – and quick. This isn't actually grasping after cash. In fact, as I'll explain, it's the least extravagant response, and a model of betting sobriety. The other ones might seem plausible, even stoical, but they're ultimately reckless.

It's all very well justifying improper risk like some game show contestant by saying 'I came with nothing and so I will be happy to leave with nothing' – until you do leave with nothing.

* * *

This scenario raises some very interesting questions and dilemmas for us in sports betting. What do you do with the profits you are making? *How will you avoid winning your way to reckless losses?*

For people operating a level-stakes system over the course of a period of time there is no financial impact on their betting other than the comfort of a bigger betting bank. If you are operating a percentage-based risk system though, as your bank grows, the physical amount of your bets will also be increasing in monetary terms (a constant as a percentage, taking the same size out of a bigger pie).

The danger for both sets of people is if the growing betting bank creates feelings of excitement and overconfidence and they decide to start betting bigger than their staking systems suggest they should.

Having a strategy for managing your betting bank and your profits is key to avoiding getting sucked into taking excessive risk or over betting because you have the money there to do it. Seeing the money you made from your betting as money to play with, for example, is a very dangerous way of thinking. Likewise, money made from big wins or unexpected results can often lead you to behaving differently in your betting.

Traditional economic theory assumes that money is fungible – that is, that any pound can be used in place of another pound. £100 in betting winnings, £100 in earnings and £100 in tax refund should have the same value, since each has the same purchasing power. People are not computers, however, and so we tend to separate our money into different mental accounts: treating £1 in one account differently from £1 in another. We have an inclination to categorise and treat money differently depending on where it comes from, where it is kept, or how it is spent. This is called mental accounting.

I have seen many people make good profits from their betting only to give it all back. They worked hard and were disciplined in growing their initial betting bank, but then mental accounting led them to behave differently, to bet differently, with this new amount. Somehow it seemed less real than the money they had started out with. Over betting and over staking soon followed, not long before a wipe out.

Managing your betting bank as it grows and monitoring your behaviour as it grows are key.

What can be done?

The most important factor in this situation is developing self-awareness that you are moving into a time of potentially higher risk. Remember that you are the greatest risk in your betting and that if your behaviours change then discipline, performance and monetary returns may all also be affected. Being aware that you are having a good run and then being aware of any signs that your attitudes or behaviours are changing is important.

We are looking for changes in attitude and behaviour as these will precede or trigger changes in performance and ultimately outcomes. This is something that I would strongly encourage anyone to do; it is why keeping records is such an important asset. During these periods, key areas that flag warnings are often when you stop doing your research and preparation or when you are not doing it as well as you could be; when you stop doing your evaluations, or again do them but with little real thought or effort; and when you start considering taking extra risk either in terms of your bet sizing or the types of bet that you are taking.

The second factor that is key is to keep focused on maintaining your winning betting approach. This can be done, as we have seen, by having a checklist of tasks and actions to perform each day and then committing to them. If you start having key tasks that cannot be ticked, or you are not even keeping the list, then these are all good warning signs.

Put it into practice: staying focused when trading is going well

1. Awareness of performance – be aware that you are on a good run; perhaps through looking at your current performance against historical performance.

2. Awareness of behaviour and mindset – monitor your betting behaviours and your mindset:

   - Have you stopped doing or reduced the quality of any of your key betting tasks?

   - Are you deviating from your betting strategy?

   - Are you wanting to take excessive risks?

   - Have you become less focused on your betting generally?

   - Are you spending more or less time betting than you do on average?

   - Have you noticed any changes in your thoughts about betting? 'This is easy'; 'I have cracked it'; 'I just can't lose', etc.

3. Control – make a list of key tasks to complete each time you bet and key aspects of betting to focus on. Keep a record of whether you actually follow through on these each day. If you are consistently following all of your betting processes then that is great. If you are not, then take that as a warning light, stop betting and re-evaluate.

Success breeds success

When betting is going well it feels great. A key reason for this is the positive emotions you are feeling and the chemical release of feel-good hormones within your body. The 'winner's high' is an interesting concept. Research into it shows that, following a win, the chemicals released in the brain create a 'high' and that the emotions that this generates leads people into ways of thinking and acting that then tend to enhance the chances of future success. If they get success again then they are in a perpetuating cycle.

When things are going well with your betting, the same is true, and a sense of momentum can be felt. It is critical to keep this momentum and maintain as much forward progress as possible to capture the opportunity whilst it is there. A key part of this process is identifying what is working and doing more of it.

Put it into practice: building on successes

Look through your logs, records and evaluations – what are you doing that is helping you to be successful right now?

What could you do more or less of that would further improve your performance?

Taking action

Now you have read this section take time to write a few notes, the key points, then consider how they apply to you in your own sports betting, before finally thinking about how you can take action.

Notes
....

How does this apply to me?
....

How can I take action?
....

10 Focus on Continual Improvement

"If I am through learning, I am through."

– John Wooden, legendary NCAA basketball coach

In this chapter:

- The path to betting success
- Kaizen
- Growth mindset
- Ways to develop your betting performance
- Raising the bar

The path to betting success

Becoming successful at sports betting is a transformational process – along the way you will change, you will develop new skills, knowledge, behaviours and mindsets. Those who do not transform, who do not make the required changes, do not achieve their full potential.

Here is a model of the pathway towards becoming consistently profitable in sports betting.

Transformational betting – three stages of sports betting development

1. Learning (beginner-novice)

- Develop required basic skills, knowledge and understanding.
- Spend time on practising basics – perhaps 'paper' betting.
- Bet with small size.
- Develop key actions and disciplines.
- Work from directed knowledge – perhaps a strategy learnt from a book or course.
- Conscious execution of skills.
- May still be naive about the challenge and difficulty of achieving betting success.
- Prone to overconfidence from any early successes in betting.

2. Consolidation (intermediate-competent)

- Beginning to personalise their betting strategy and style.

- Ongoing development of skills, knowledge and understanding.

- Skills becoming more unconscious (automatic) through repetition and practice.

- Likely to have encountered periods of loss and losses that have tested their commitment, self-belief and resilience.

- Developing awareness of importance of psychology in betting.

3. Mastery (expert-master)

- Has the skill and ability to develop and execute strategy in line with own abilities, skills, strengths and preferred risk, decision-making, information-processing and behavioural styles.

- Extensive levels of unconscious competence.

- Continual improvement is a focus.

- Flexible and adaptable to changing market and personal circumstances.

- Able to, if prepared and willing, coach and mentor other people.

- Experienced – 'weathered' – in the betting markets.

- Fully understands and pays attention to the importance of psychology in achieving consistent betting performance.

- Less focused on just making or losing money, and more focused on process, decision-making and mastering one's craft.

* * *

Although I have give three categories here, we are really looking at a continuum of development as shown in the diagram below.

The betting development continuum

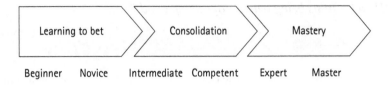

Beginner Novice	Intermediate Competent	Expert Master

"My journey to becoming a successful full-time sports bettor is built upon hours and hours of studying the various markets and devising systems that work for me"

– Pete Nordsted

 Review: where are you on the continuum?

Take some time to look at the model and reflect on where you are currently.

Where do you feel your key areas for development are right now?

What action can you take to address them?

One of the most important aspects to observe is that movement along the continuum is dependent on learning and development, but most crucially that even at the far right, at mastery, continual improvement is a key focus. Sports betting continues to evolve, with new sports to bet on, new markets, new software, new systems and opportunities; evolution requires adaptation, and that means learning.

Kaizen

"He who stops being better stops being good."

– Oliver Cromwell

The Japanese have a word for the concept of continual improvement: kaizen. Kaizen is a philosophy that Japanese business has been built upon and is a concept which is evident across the world in top sports people and teams, businesses, traders and – yes – sports bettors.

The most successful people I have met in sports betting are still learning and developing. They are focused on continuing to improve. They are always working towards being the best they can be, learning from their experience, building on their strengths, learning new skills and approaches and letting go of things that are not working. This is mastery in action.

The rage to master

In his research on developing expertise, K. Anders Eriksson identified a "rage to master" amongst people who achieved expertise – an insatiable desire for knowledge and development. For example, in chess he found an interesting correlation between a player's rating (Grand Master etc.) and the number of books, videos and resources they owned on chess.

Continual improvement does not happen by accident. It is a process. It requires you to evaluate what you have done, to learn from that and to use it to improve your performance. A powerful question to ask yourself at the end of any betting session is 'What have I learnt?'

There are, however, some challenges to be aware of in maintaining continual improvement. Including:

- complacency
- the illusion of mastery

- loss of enthusiasm

- becoming stagnant.

Keeping an awareness of these and noticing when your focus shifts away from learning and development is important.

Development, learning and performance improvement

If you wanted to learn to play golf, fly a plane, play the piano, drive a car or to cook, what would you do? The majority of people would perhaps consider getting some lessons. And if you wanted to become *highly* successful in those areas, then training and education would be foremost in your mind. Training, coaching and mentoring can all enable you to develop your betting performance more quickly, or beyond the point you could get to purely with your own resources.

> *"I would suggest that people read everything they can, join forums, get amongst other traders and practise what they learn. Watch all the videos you can. Surround yourself with people that do what you do as otherwise it can be a very lonely existence."*
>
> – Tony Hargraves

Commit to excellence for an improved betting performance and a better life

"The quality of a person's life is in direct proportion to his commitment to excellence, regardless of their chosen field".
– Vince Lombardi, American football coach

The four key components of sports trading

To become successful in sports betting you need to develop your abilities in four key areas:

1. Analysis – being able to analyse and identify betting opportunities.

2. Strategy – knowing which strategies to apply and when, and in which markets.

3. Risk management – knowing how much to risk; your staking plan.

4. Discipline – sticking to your plan and dealing with the ups and downs of trading.

When you are looking at your key areas of development it is useful to ensure that you are addressing your needs across all four areas.

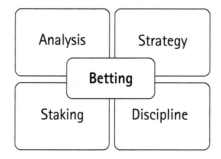

Review: development needs assessment

Very quickly rate your ability in each of the four components out of ten, where ten is the best you feel you could be.

Area	Ability
Analysis	
Strategy	
Risk management	
Discipline	

What are your individual component scores?

What is your overall score?

In each area list your strengths, and then your areas for improvement.

From your list of areas to improve, prioritise them in order of which would be most useful to address in having an impact on your betting performance.

Finally, decide what you need to do to work on your targeted areas and achieve the outcome you want.

Training

Good quality training is critical to achieving success in betting, just as it is in any other high performance area.

Training should be structured appropriately to meet the needs of the person. It should involve a relevant curriculum of study, with continuity and progression running throughout. Ideally there will be opportunities to practise, to try out ideas and learn the basics of execution either on a simulator or live in the markets.

A key feature of all training programmes should be the opportunity to get regular feedback, as this is critical to quality learning experiences. It is powerful in accelerating development.

The quality of a training programme can have a massive impact on your betting career and can launch you onto the path of either success or failure.

For most people, training typically occurs at the beginning of their betting career and is founded on teaching the core basics, enabling them to engage in the markets with competence. However, it is important to stay in the learning loop and to keep updating your market knowledge, to look at new betting methodologies or to develop your psychology and performance skills.

Key aspects of a good quality training programme:

- relevant curriculum
- continuity
- progression
- duration
- feedback – regular and of a high quality
- simulation

- live betting
- expert and experienced tutors with trading experience/success
- assessment
- lots of opportunities for interacting with the tutors
- development post-training – mentoring/coaching opportunities.

Mentoring

Mentoring is a process that goes right back in history and has stood the test of time as a very effective process for developing a person's competence in a given field.

Mentoring from a more experienced person can be a very powerful experience when it is carried out correctly. It can have a significant impact on the speed and quality of your learning.

The relationship between the mentor and the mentored has to be defined. Both parties need to know what the aims and outcomes of the relationship are and how the process will work. For the mentored, having someone to watch bet, to watch you bet, to bounce ideas and questions off, is extremely important. For the mentor, there are also benefits. I have found that in mentoring someone you have to consolidate your own understanding of what you are doing. You develop new skills in communication. And you also get the immense satisfaction of watching your 'student' grow and develop.

What to look for in a mentor:

- experience
- knowledge
- actual betting history
- communication skills
- commitment to students
- time and availability.

Interestingly, over time the mentored can become the mentor, as their skills and knowledge become greater. You are then sought out by other people, and are able to pass on your experience to others (should you wish to). For me this is a natural part of one's development, and certainly worth doing.

Psychological coaching

Discipline is key to achieving success in sports betting, as we talked about earlier in the book. And for a lot of people, a lack of it is a barrier to them achieving greater profitability or consistency.

People often recognise that they have a problem with their discipline. However, unlike with developing a new betting strategy or staking plans, there is little support out there beyond people's stories and advice on forums.

Where discipline is a challenge, and particularly for those people who have a strategy with an edge and some experience with betting, psychological coaching can help to make the shifts in mindset, emotional response and behaviour required to move onwards and upwards.

Psychological coaching

For information on how to get support with improving your betting discipline and psychological challenges, contact the author through www.highperformanceglobal.com

---

Practice

If you want to get better at anything then you need to practise. But practice alone is not good enough. K. Anders Eriksson has identified the need for *deliberate practice* if someone is to achieve a high level of performance.

Deliberate practice is different in that the practice session has a distinct focus and that feedback is provided about the performance. This is different from more casual practice or play. This may account for why, after 25 years of playing the guitar, I have not progressed beyond the most basic of playing abilities. It is not *how much* practice you do, but how you practise that counts.

Deliberate practice is different in that the practice session has a distinct focus and that feedback is provided about the performance.

Committing to practising new skills, techniques and strategies will help you to develop your betting. It is important to stress, though, that when you are practising you should reduce your risk accordingly and do so in low-key events, where the outcome is not as significant for you.

Reading and watching videos

Reading books and articles and watching videos can all be good ways of developing your knowledge and understanding, of developing new strategies and keeping you growing. They are accessible and often affordable ways of learning, with the one key drawback being the lack of feedback you get from them and the inability to ask questions and get clarification.

Networking

Professionals in sports betting often have a good network of people around them who they can bounce ideas off, talk with and share banter with through the day. Tony Hargraves recommends that people find a "buddy" to be able to do this with, as betting from home can be a solitary experience.

Jack Canfield, in his book *Success Principles,* states that you are the sum of the five people who you spend the most time with. Who are the five people you spend the most time with? What is the impact of this on your sports betting? Ideally what five people would you spend your time with? What steps can you take to move towards this?

Developing your own network of like-minded individuals can be a very powerful way of advancing your betting over time.

> *"There is a big advantage for traders in a trading environment in information flow. They are surrounded by experts, and they have likeminded people to bounce ideas off. People trading from home don't have that environment or interaction."*

> – Ian Massie

Put it into practice: develop your trading network

Which five people would spending time with most help your betting performance?

Keep raising the bar, and learn and earn more

"Champions never ask whether or not it is possible to raise the bar on their performance. The question they ask is 'How is it possible; what do I have to do?'"

– Jerry Lynch, *The Way of the Champion*

One of the key philosophies that I aim to pass on in my own training and coaching is *learning and earning more*. The two cannot be dissociated. Keep focused on learning, because as you learn more so your potential to earn more grows.

Here are a few pointers to focus on to keep you learning:

Put your attention on trying to be better than you currently are. Keep asking yourself 'How can I improve my betting performance? What do I have to do?'

Keep taking small steps forward – do not underestimate the power of taking many small steps.

Be teachable and coachable – be open to new experiences, to new ideas and concepts. Socrates said: "My wisdom lay in this; unlike other men I know how ignorant I am."

From poacher to gamekeeper, from punter to sports trader

"I started with an interest in sport and became a casual punter before trying to take things more seriously. Since I have been at Spreadex I have been able to continually improve my own betting. This is particularly down to seeing the mistakes and the resulting losses that people are making and by being in an environment where I am surrounded by really knowledgeable people, experts, and great sports traders."

– Ian Massie

Taking action

Now you have read this section take time to write a few notes, the key points, then consider how they apply to you in your own sports betting, before finally thinking about how you can take action.

Notes

How does this apply to me?

How can I take action?

Extra Time – Going Pro: Sports Betting Full Time

"It is a massive psychological leap to give up the security of a full-time job to do sports betting full time."

– Tony Hargraves

In this chapter:

- Important considerations before going full time

- Making the move – the transition to full-time betting

- Living the life – full-time betting practicalities

Important considerations

Is this really what you want to do?

For most people who are committed to their sports betting, there comes a point where they start to ask themselves 'Could I do this full time?', 'Could I become a professional?'

The key question to consider alongside whether you could do it full time is 'Do I really want to do this full time?'

Taking the step to betting full time is a big one, particularly if it means leaving full-time employment. There are many factors that you should take into account before doing so. It is a decision that should not be taken too lightly or too quickly.

Sports betting full time is in reality not always what people perceive it to be. And whilst there are definite attractions in terms of the financial gains, freedom and opportunities, there are also aspects to solemnly consider, such as having no regular income and having to endure periods of drawdown (loss). Not all people are cut out for being self-employed.

Are you good enough?

Professionals in any area of activity are so called because they make their living from what they do. And, of course, the nature and standard of this living can vary significantly. A key question you have to ask yourself is 'Am I good enough to do this full time for a living?'

Have you demonstrated over a significant period of time that you are disciplined and can perform with consistency and generate good results?

- Do you understand why you are winning and losing?

- Can you make enough money from your betting to support the lifestyle you have or want?

- What is your expected return/income?

- What hours will you work?

- What is this as an hourly rate?

- Do you have a sufficiently big enough betting bank to allow you to make the return you need without taking high risk?

- Do you have sufficient starting capital to provide a buffer over the first few months and to endure any periods where your earnings are below your needs?

- Do you have a plan?

- Have you developed your betting plan?

Remember that you are effectively starting a betting business, so start by producing your 'business plan' and assessing the viability of your venture.

Are you disciplined enough?

Here I am talking more about the self-discipline required to run your own business and work from home. Being self-employed has many advantages and the freedom to choose your own hours is one of those. However, it also means that there is no one apart from you to set those hours and make sure that you are putting in the required time. On the flipside of this, is not getting drawn into betting on everything just because you now have the time to.

Running your own business and working from home takes self-discipline. Have you got it?

How will you cope when times are tough?

It is inevitable that you will have good times and not-so-good times with your betting. Ensuring that you have the capability both financially and mentally to deal with such periods is important.

How will you feel if you lose money one month? Two months in a row?

How would you cope financially if you couldn't pay yourself from your betting one month, or maybe even two, or longer?

Being financially and psychologically resilient is essential.

What are the implications for those around you?

> "Betting successfully will inevitably have a considerable impact upon your personal life both in terms of time spent and in terms of financial resources. The same is true of unsuccessful betting.
>
> "It goes without saying that you should consult fully with any person in your life who will be affected by your actions."
>
> – Keith Sobey

For people with families, taking into account the impact of your move to full-time betting is a very important one.

If you are now going to be working from home what are the implications here?

If you are sacrificing a regular income, what is the impact of that?

What is the back-up plan?

When people start on new ventures they are naturally keen and enthusiastic and it is full-steam ahead. However, it is sensible to give some consideration to what would be your back up plan if full-time sports betting didn't work out for you.

How long will you give yourself to decide whether it is working or not?

What will the evidence – either way – be?

Age concern

"Age is an important consideration for people who are looking at giving up work to bet full time. For someone in their late twenties/early thirties it is possible to give it a try and then if it doesn't work out they still have a good possibility of getting back into a regular job. For someone in their fifties, the outlook is not quite the same. So the prospects of what happens if I don't make it should be very carefully considered."

– Peter Webb

Making the move

Moving into sports betting full-time is a transition, either from studying, working or unemployment. Getting this transition right is important in ensuring that, once you are ready to make the move, it is made as effectively as possible.

If you are working full-time and betting part-time then the obvious transition appears to be just to go into full-time trading. This, however, means committing fully to full-time betting and leaving full-time work behind, without having ever experienced the realities of full-time betting. It can be quite different betting part-time, and an aptitude at one does not guarantee an (immediate) aptitude at the other.

An approach that I have encouraged people to take in transitioning from betting part-time to full-time is to take some time off work as a paid holiday or unpaid (this can give you a longer time period and create a more realistic environment) to experience life as a full-time better. During this period I would encourage the person to replicate as much as possible what betting full time will be like; this would include the working hours, lifestyle factors, dress code. This can help to give another insight into the benefits and challenges of betting full time.

A two-week period may not be long enough to get over the initial excitement of betting full time but it will provide some insights. If you can get four weeks then it will give you a much better flavour. However, nothing can ultimately prepare you for the reality of sports betting full time.

Psychological factors to consider

Making the transition to sports betting full time does bring with it some psychological considerations.

If you are sports betting full time you are essentially self-employed. Self-employment has many great advantages and it is why so many people like to own their own businesses. However, there are some important things that need to be considered:

- Freedom – you will have more freedom to do what you want, when you want it. BUT you will need the self-discipline to do what you need to do when you need to do it.

- Income – you will no longer be guaranteed a regular monthly income. The amount that you make from your betting can vary greatly from month to month. Psychologically this level of uncertainty can be unsettling and stressful for many people, especially if historically you have always had regular pay cheques.

- Employment benefits – you may have enjoyed employment benefits such as a pension, holiday pay and sick pay, maybe even healthcare and gym memberships. Can you provide these with your new betting lifestyle? Which are you ready to let go of?

- Pressure to perform. If you don't make money you don't eat. Many people come into full-time sports betting having worked full time and bet part time initially, perhaps as a hobby, and then in more serious form and perhaps generating a second income. They feel that, because they have made a good secondary income from sports betting, having more time and energy to devote to it would generate a good full-time income. This is not always the case. When people have the security of a first income the pressure of creating profits from the secondary betting income is not there. When the primary income is betting it is a very different situation psychologically. You have to generate profits from your betting which you can live on. Ensuring that you have adequate capital to live on in the early stages of your betting career is critical, and keeping three to six months worth of living money is always a good strategy to see you through tough times and take the pressure off. Nothing is worse than placing bets because you have to make money.

Matt makes the move

"My reason for making the move to becoming a full-time sports trader was that I wanted to own time. Money wasn't my drive. I was fed up of working the corporate ladder and I made the decision at 31 that it wasn't the life for me.

"I worked out the minimum that I required to live on each month without all the usual materialistic luxuries of my lifestyle and decided the 60-70 hours a week I was spending as company spokesman for Ladbrokes would be better spent learning a new trade.

"It wasn't easy and during my apprenticeship there were tough times – losing my bank, having to take interim work to start again – but in 2005 (three years after I set out) I finally had the understanding and confidence to sustain long-term profits.

"Less than five years after leaving Ladbrokes I achieved the ultimate goal of leading a debt-free life of no mortgage etc.

"I know my current lifestyle wouldn't have been possible if I hadn't made the choice to follow my passion and dream. My world is recession-proof. Man United will always play Arsenal or Chelsea and I know that when they do I can make money on it!"

– Matt Finnigan

Peter's bumpy start

"I made the move to full-time sports betting based on two primary drivers:

I had always wanted to work for myself; and

I was fed up with corporate work.

"I remember how difficult I found it transitioning from having a regular income to not having one, and I think it took me about 12-18 months to really feel comfortable. It helped that I had 18 months of money put away for me to experiment with.

"The early part of that move away from full-time employment took a lot of mental strength. No one took me seriously. Everyone thought I was a fool. To be honest, when I started I didn't know if anyone else was doing this and making a living from it. I started trading on Betfair just seven days after it opened and I saw that there was an opportunity there. I decided to make the jump. I spoke with the wife and then left work forever.

"There were a few bumpy days and months at the start but after a while it settled into a bit of a pattern."

– Peter Webb

Living the life – full-time betting practicalities

When you are betting full time for a living you are the boss and you have to set the parameters for creating a working environment and lifestyle that meets your needs and objectives.

Some aspects to consider are covered in this section.

Creating a conducive betting environment

Where you work, your environment can have a significant impact on your performance. Take some time to create the best possible working environment for yourself.

One thing that I would certainly recommend where appropriate and possible is having a separate working desk/area. This is important in helping the mind to focus on the required task at hand with minimal external distraction.

What can you do to maximise the effectiveness of your working environment?

Dress code

Many people look forward to escaping full-time employment because of freedom and one of those freedoms is being able to wear what you want. However, it is important to consider what you will wear whilst you are betting, because it can have an impact on your performance. It can be all too easy when working from home to not actually get dressed into any kind of daytime attire and to spend the day betting at the PC in your boxer shorts, unshaven and without having showered.

What will you wear that enables you to be at your best?

Working hours

When you are self-employed there are no working hours except those that you set for yourself. It is important to have in your mind an understanding of the hours that you will be working, from both the perspective of doing enough hours to generate the income you need but also being mindful of the ease with which you can fall into the 'bet on anything' mentality and end up working excessive hours that may actually be detrimental to your profitability.

You will also want to think about holidays, weekends and evenings and how you manage to ensure you get sufficient time and rest away from betting. Tony Hargraves says that "I aim to have a maximum of 24 days each month when I am trading and then for the other six days I try and get right away from it all and switch off. You need to get away; if you don't you'll just burn out."

Betting for a living can be unsociable

"As a married man with two small children, finding the time to bet is difficult as sports are on at quite unsociable hours like evenings and weekends."

– Tony Hargraves

Creating a network

"Surround yourself with the right people in a healthy environment."

– Jerry Lynch, *The Way of the Champion*

Betting from home has many advantages. It can also be quite lonely. Developing a network of people who you can communicate with, perhaps share ideas with, and just talk to, is very important.

Who you choose to be in this network is also important. You are putting together a team of people to help you to achieve your best possible betting results. Who would you want in that team? Some people may be in it for ideas/information, others for support, others for purely social reasons, but none the less each has their purpose. Be careful when building your team that you choose people who add to your success and are not the sort of people who can bring negativity to the table.

"Get a betting buddy who you can bounce some ideas off and chat to if you feel like being on your own all day is going to drive you insane."

– Tony Hargraves

Managing your money

When you start betting full time it can be an excellent idea, if you have not done it already, to have a separate account for your betting. This is in effect your business account, and allows you to see with great transparency your available funds and your cash flow.

How to avoid muddling the housekeeping money and your betting bank

"I set up a new bank account, in which I deposited the money I was prepared to trade with. That means, at the end of each week, month, year, I know exactly what I have won and lost. I even withdraw cash, when I am going to the races, from the same account. You'll never get a clear idea of how good or bad a trader you are if you get the housekeeping money muddled up with the trading pot!"

– Bill Esdaile

Work-life balance

"The extent of your fulfilment and success is directly related to the balance you create among the nutritional, social, familial, professional, physical, mental and emotional-spiritual aspects of your life."

– Jerry Lynch, *Thinking Body, Dancing Mind*

Is there life outside of betting for you?

What is that life?

How do you spend your time outside of betting?

What role do you play apart from being a sports better? Parent, friend, athlete, artist?

Betting professionally is a fantastic occupation. It is not only challenging, interesting and enjoyable but it can also offer the opportunity to live a great lifestyle. However, it is also demanding in terms of time and energy. Balance and diversity can alleviate the incredible and real pressure of betting for a living. If betting is the most important thing in your life and is your sole focus, then your biggest challenge is that, when betting is going well, life is great, but when betting is not going well, life is not great. That is – that betting and life are positively correlated and that your life happiness is largely dictated by your betting results. This is not healthy.

When you have interests outside of betting it means that all your happiness eggs are not in one basket and that when times are tough in betting, you can be getting your needed doses of happiness and positive energy from other areas.

"You need to dovetail betting successfully with your personal life if you are to become a lifelong winner."

– Keith Sobey

Routines and rituals

It can be very useful to consider and establish for yourself some core routines that enable you to manage your lifestyle and your betting and get the best out of both. Here are some areas where you may wish to establish routines – some, as you will see, are directly attributable to your betting performance, whilst others have more of a knock-on and supportive effect.

In *Stress for Success* by James Loehr, the following ten rituals are identified as being the most important in terms of performance lifestyle.

1. Sleep – consistent patterns for getting up and going to bed protect the sleep cycle. Going to bed early and waking up early works for most performers,

2. Exercise – daily exposure to exercise of some kind is important to overall balance.

3. Nutrition – the timing, frequency and content of your meals are extremely important.

4. Family – time with family grounds you, creates bonds and affirms meaning in your life.

5. Spirituality – spiritual time heals you, confirming your purpose and essentials in life – a foundation for personal growth.

6. Preperformance – like tennis players and golfers before serving or putting, in betting we need concrete preparation routines.

7. Travel – to gain control over your emotional response to traffic or train as and if appropriate.

8. Office – the in-between time in betting is critical to success. It's time for recovery and then preparation. Taking small 'energy-breaks' such as eating a healthy snack; leaving your desk for a walk around – fresh air, even a walk up and down a flight of stairs; then allowing yourself a few minutes for your 'prep' ritual before you begin your next bet.

9. Creative time – playing a musical instrument, creative writing, artistic pursuits, etc. can all play a critical role in balancing stress.

10. Home – creating home-rituals to wind down after a day's betting reenergises and is just as important as getting psyched or being fired up to perform.

Enjoying it all

If you are betting full time for a living and overall it is going to plan, then remember to enjoy it. It is easy to get caught up in the highs and lows of betting, to get consumed with the processes of betting, to stress and worry about performance, and to forget about the many positives, the benefits that life as a full-time pro brings.

Take time each day to remind yourself of what you are grateful for.

Did you win or lose?

"My grandfather (who I never met) was a ferocious punter. However, my grandmother said that she could never tell whether he won or lost when he went to the races. She said that he often brought her home a present when he turned out to have won, and often brought her home a present when he turned out to have lost. So she could never tell. In short, it is so important that sports betting doesn't alter your personality away from the game."

– Bill Esdaile

Appendix – The OODA Model

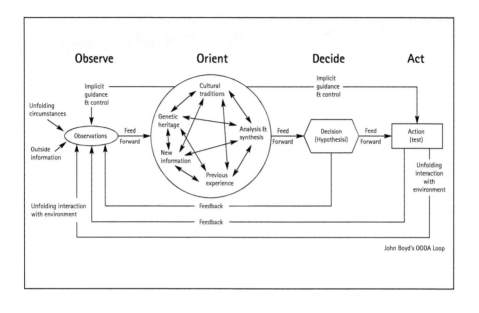

Bibliography

Belsky, Gary and Gilovich, Thomas, *Why Smart People Make Big Money Mistakes and How to Correct Them* (Simon and Schuster, 1999)

Canfield, Jack, *The Success Principles* (HarperCollins, 2005)

Childre, Doc and Martin, Howard, *The Heartmath Solution* (Harper, 1999)

Douglas, Mark, *The Disciplined Trader* (Penguin Putnam, 1990)

Douglas, Mark, *Trading in the Zone* (Prentice Hall, 2000)

Dweck, Carol S., *Mindset* (Random House, 2006)

Ericsson, K. Anders, *The Road to Excellence* (Lawrence Erlbaum, 1996)

Erikkson, Sven-Göran, *Sven Göran Eriksson on Football* (Carlton Books, 2002)

Gallwey, W. Timothy, *The Inner Game of Golf* (Pan Books, 1979)

Gladwell, Malcolm, *Blink* (Penguin, 2006)

Gladwell, Malcolm, *Outliers* (Penguin, 2009)

Gowar, Alex and Houghton, Jack, *Winning on Betfair for Dummies* (John Wiley & Sons, 2008)

Hodges, Jeffrey, *Champion Thoughts Champion Feelings* (Sportsmind Institute, 1998)

Kealy, Paul, *The Definitive Guide to Betting Exchanges* (Raceform Ltd, 2005)

Loehr, James E., *Stress for Success* (Random House, 1997)

Lynch, Jerry, *The Way of the Champion* (Tuttle, 2006)

Lynch, Jerry and Huang, Chungliang Al, *Thinking Body, Dancing Mind* (Bantam, 1992)

Millington, Bruce, *The Definitive Guide to Betting on Sports* (Raceform Ltd, 2004)

Murphy, Shane and Hirschborn, Doug, *The Trading Athlete* (Wiley, 2001)

Schwager, Jack D., *Market Wizards* (Collins, 1993)

Seligman, Martin E.P., *Learned Optimism* (Free Press, 1990)

Shinar, Yehuda, *Think Like a Winner* (Vermillion, 2007)

Steenbarger, Brett N., *Enhancing Trader Performance* (Wiley, 2007)

Ward, Steve, *High Performance Trading* (Harriman House, 2009)

Zweig, Jason, *Your Money and Your Brain* (Simon and Schuster, 2007)

Index

A

account management, 181

addictive gambling, 27

adrenaline rush, 14–15, 76, 114

anger, 78, 112, 129

anxiety, 120

attitude. *see* mindset

attribution theory, 100–101

B

back-up plans, 175

balance sheet, 34

behaviour, betting, 25–28, 56, 62, 63

behaviour, human, 74–75

    emotions, 77–79, 82, 120-121

behavioural finance, 75

betting development continuum, 159

betting exchanges, 35

bookies, 16, 35

bookmakers. *see* bookies

boredom, 77, 106–107

business planning, 34–35, 38, 174

C

casual betting, 27, 33

'clusters', 139

coaching, 161, 166

cognition, 81

commitment, 29

competence, 128

competitive advantage, 42–44

composure, 49

concentration, 50

confidence, 78, 120, 126–129. *see also*
        overconfidence

confirmation bias, 76–77

consistency, 49

control, 49

costs. *see* expenditure

critical moments, 132–134

D

data, 64, 83

decision-making, 13–14, 62, 63

    behavioural finance, 75

    disciplined, 83

    intuitive, 81

    Observe Orient Decide Act model,
        73–75, 185

    process, 80

    rational, 84–87

development, personal, 157–159

discipline, 63, 83, 128, 162–163

    coaching for, 166

    and self-employment, 174

9 780857 190390